Once a Jolly Swagman

Waltzing Matilda Country

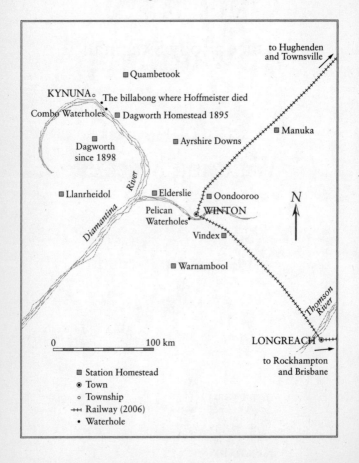

■ Quambetook

KYNUNA ○ The billabong where Hoffmeister died

Combo Waterholes • ■ Dagworth Homestead 1895

■ Ayrshire Downs

■ Manuka

■
Dagworth
since 1898

■ Llanrheidol   ■ Elderslie   ■ Oondooroo

Pelican ⊙ WINTON
Waterholes

■ Vindex

Diamantina River

N

■ Warnambool

0 _____ 100 km

LONGREACH ⊙

Thomson River

to Hughenden
and Townsville

to Rockhampton
and Brisbane

■ Station Homestead
⊙ Town
○ Township
+++ Railway (2006)
• Waterhole

Once a Jolly Swagman

The Ballad of Waltzing Matilda

Matthew Richardson

MELBOURNE
UNIVERSITY
PRESS

The Publishers would like to thank Dave de Hugard for allowing the use of his rendition of 'Waltzing Matilda' from the original Christina MacPherson manuscript. The song can also be found on Dave's CD, 'Songs of the Wallaby Track'. If you would like more information on Dave and his music, please go to www.dehugard.com.

MELBOURNE UNIVERSITY PRESS
An imprint of Melbourne University Publishing Ltd
187 Grattan Street, Carlton, Victoria 3053, Australia
mup-info@unimelb.edu.au
www.mup.com.au

First published 2006
Text © Matthew Richardson 2006
Design and typography © Melbourne University Publishing Ltd
2006

Designed by Melanie Feddersen
Edited by Wendy Skilbeck
Typeset in Sabon by TypeSkill
Printed in Australia by McPherson's Printing Group

National Library of Australian Cataloguing-in-Publication entry
Richardson, Matthew.
    Once a jolly swagman : the ballad of Waltzing Matilda.
    ISBN 9780522853087.
    ISBN 0 522 85308 0.

1. Waltzing Matilda. 2. Songs, English – Australia.
3. National songs – Australia – History and criticism.
4. Folklore – Australia. 5. National characteristics,
Australian. I. Title.

782.4215990269

Background to chapter headings: A.B. 'Banjo' Paterson's handwritten words to 'Waltzing Matilda', 1895.

Contents

A Note to the Reader

Vol. I in references throughout the book stands for *Singer of the Bush*, the first volume of *A. B. 'Banjo' Paterson: Complete Works*; Vol. II is *Song of the Pen*, the second volume of *A. B. 'Banjo' Paterson: Complete Works*.

The recording enclosed in this edition is Dave de Hugard's rendition of 'Waltzing Matilda' using Christina Macpherson's original tune, and lyrics composed by Banjo Paterson, when they created the song in Queensland in 1895. It represents the song as it would have sounded in its first years.

PREFACE

In 1895 Japan was waging war on China. The Lumière brothers turned a Paris café into the first cinema, and Sigmund Freud published his work on psychoanalysis. South Australian women were granted the right to run for Parliament. Six Australian colonies were preparing for Federation, but still ran as separate countries, with the British crown their only political bond. The economic depression was starting to ease.

In western Queensland, Christina Macpherson of Melbourne—Chris to those who knew her— met the poet A. B. Paterson—Banjo to his readers. Neither was a songwriter but together they created 'Waltzing Matilda'.

Soon after Banjo's return to Sydney, *The Man from Snowy River and Other Verses* was launched, ever to be the most popular book of Australian poetry. A varied career placed Paterson in the roles of bushman, lawyer, correspondent, folklorist, editor, traveller, grazier and officer. In a dashing manner not typical of poets and lawyers, he took on hazardous adventures such as buffalo hunting in the Territory and combat reporting from the front line.

Strong forces worked against Banjo Paterson's renown. Being conspicuously distant and modest, he didn't promote his name. Critics slighted his poetry, and schools and universities mostly ignored it. But among his fellow Australians these forces were weak compared to their love of his work. Throughout the continent, the Man from Snowy River is a household word today; around the world 'Waltzing Matilda' is recognised as Australia's favourite song. Banjo's aloof gaze meets the eyes of millions, from paintings, illustrations, statues and $10 notes.

Chris Macpherson went back to Victoria after a brief residence on her family's Queensland station. She was well educated, good at music, and good looking; but all we really know is that she lived obscurely in Melbourne for the remainder of her life, single and unrecognised. So far as I'm aware, no painting or monument honours her, not even a postage stamp. At least she is credited in books for her creative contribution to 'Waltzing Matilda', as are other little known persons who appear in the chapters to come.

It seems odd to be writing a whole book about a song, though I'm not alone in that respect. You might find a book about 'Lili Marlene' for instance, or 'Danny Boy'. There have been Waltzing Matilda books since 1944.

Peculiar songs, these—sung all over the world and translated into many languages, but strongly identified with their homelands. Nothing in them is implicitly patriotic, competitive or jingoistic, yet each kindles even in cynics a passionate enthusiasm for their country and people.

Previous books about 'Waltzing Matilda' concentrate on its provenance and political background. Now, thanks to previous work, it's easy to tell the story of the song's creation as a good yarn, rather than a controversy muddled by contradictory leads. It's also time to contemplate the effects of 'Waltzing Matilda' as a phenomenon in a century and more since it was first sung.

The world changes a lot in a century: some things arrive brand new; some, including swagmen, virtually disappear. Other things go full circle. One hears that in today's multicultural society old constants of Australian culture no longer belong. Yet the people of Australia are more homogenous now than after the Gold Rushes, when so many were still struggling with English. When 'Waltzing Matilda' was born, immigrants were still a higher proportion in the population than they are now, especially in country areas.

Some special things don't change much in the changing world. Since 'Waltzing Matilda' soared in popularity, thousands of songs have done likewise. But as each one then fades into obscurity, 'Waltzing Matilda' remains, the perennial hit.

***

I have read that when children are young, parents should sing to them. I tried it on my own children, but soon after I began, they always begged me to stop. 'Waltzing Matilda' is the only song I was allowed to sing to the end, every verse and every chorus. Afterwards they said 'Can you sing that again please?'

Many reasons are given for the enduring hold of that song: it is the anthem of the underdog; or the song that makes you understand what it is to be Australian; or its rollicking melody and flowing syllables are irresistible. These may be good reasons, but, with its deep grip on every generation, even when sung badly, it will take more than a few reasonable sentences to account for the phenomenon of 'Waltzing Matilda'.

M. E. Richardson

WALTZING MATILDA
CARRYING A SWAG

Oh there once was a swagman camped in the billabongs,
　　Under the shade of a Coolibah tree;
And he sang as he looked at the old billy boiling,
　　'Who'll come a-waltzing Matilda with me.'

Who'll come a-waltzing Matilda, my darling,
　　Who'll come a-waltzing Matilda with me.
Waltzing Matilda and leading a water-bag,
　　Who'll come a-waltzing Matilda with me.

Up came the jumbuck to drink at the waterhole,
　　Up jumped the swagman and grabbed him in glee;
And he said as he put him away in the tucker-bag,
　　'You'll come a-waltzing Matilda with me.'

You'll come a-waltzing Matilda, my darling,
　　Who'll come a-waltzing Matilda with me.
Waltzing Matilda and leading a water-bag,
　　You'll come a-waltzing Matilda with me.

Up came the squatter a-riding his thoroughbred;
　　Up came policemen—one, two, and three.
'Whose is the jumbuck you've got in the tucker-bag?
　　You'll come a-waltzing Matilda with we.'

You'll come a-waltzing Matilda, my darling,
　　Who'll come a-waltzing Matilda with me.
Waltzing Matilda and leading a water-bag,
　　You'll come a-waltzing Matilda with me.

Up sprang the swagman and jumped in the waterhole,
    Drowning himself by the Coolibah tree;
And his voice can be heard as it sings in the billabongs,
    'Who'll come a-waltzing Matilda with me.'

Who'll come a-waltzing Matilda, my darling,
    Who'll come a-waltzing Matilda with me.
Waltzing Matilda and leading a water-bag,
    Who'll come a-waltzing Matilda with me.

                                        Banjo Paterson, 1895

WALTZING MATILDA COUNTRY

FROM TASMANIA TO THE KIMBERLEYS every Australian can lay claim to 'Waltzing Matilda'. Australians identify with it wherever they go in the world. But there is one part of Queensland that has a stronger sense of proprietorship—it can truly claim to be the birthplace of 'Waltzing Matilda'.

The grasslands out beyond Longreach seem to go on forever in a series of flats and gentle slopes, dressed here and there with little trees. In fact they are punctuated by erratic rivers that take their rise in low hills; rivers that run during the wet season in a multitude of shallow courses, then shrink away into seemingly random billabongs in the dry.

From Easter till Christmas the endless sky is bright, the nights are cool and the soil is hard and dry. But every year, usually in January, the hot air turns muggy and the sky fills with grey clouds—

scrag ends of the monsoon that crosses the Gulf of Carpentaria in violent tempests, but peters out as it approaches the Tropic of Capricorn in western Queensland. Then, in a good year, it rains quietly for hours, day after day, so the plains are sodden, the grass grows suddenly, tracks turn to glue and rivers become impassable barriers, kilometres wide.

Longreach is 685 km inland, on the Tropic of Capricorn, near where it intersects the Thomson River. Downstream, the Thomson joins the Barcoo. After a particularly wet season, water from these rivers pours down Coopers Creek and into Lake Eyre.

The road that leads north-west from Longreach, the Landsborough Highway, crosses the flat country for 180 km to Winton, and beyond that takes a line not far from the course of the Diamantina River, to Kynuna. It continues out of the district across the McKinley Hills to Cloncurry. Like the Thomson River, the Diamantina carries its seasonal flow towards Lake Eyre.

Left of the highway are the vestiges of the old Cobb and Co. coach road from Winton to Kynuna, keeping low, near the river and a water supply.

For countless years this district was familiar only to ancestors of the Koa and Wanamara Aborigines. Even natives of neighbouring districts seem to have been poorly informed. Owing to the hard seasons, Aboriginal inhabitants were few—prosperous in good seasons, but depending in tough times on advanced bushcraft to eke out a meagre living.

What brought outsiders to visit was the disappearance of the explorers Burke and Wills. After crossing Australia south to north in 1861, they died coming back. When they failed to reappear, more capable explorers set out to attempt a rescue.

John McKinlay, born in Scotland in 1819, had worked in the Australian bush since the age of seventeen. In 1861 he led a party north from Adelaide, till he learnt that others had found the graves of Burke and Wills. But being well provisioned to carry on their trip, his party carried on, to places further north, battling up the boggy banks of a waterway they christened Mueller's Creek. Mueller's Creek is known now as the Diamantina River. It was renamed by the Queenslanders after Countess Diamantina Roma, Governor Bowen's wife, from Greece. At a point south-west of Winton, McKinlay left the river and carried on north-west, almost to the coast of the Gulf of Carpentaria.

In 1862 another Scotsman, William Landsborough (1825–86), came south from the Gulf, east of today's Winton, to where Longreach is now, and then across to the Barcoo. In 1865 Landsborough sat briefly in the Queensland Parliament before being appointed government representative in Burketown, in the far north-west. From there in 1866 he set out on explorations that penetrated into the heart of Waltzing Matilda country around Winton and the upper reaches of the Diamantina. He reported on the grazing potential of the district, and after a few years settlers began droving their stock in and occupying pastoral leases.

In 1875 Robert Allen opened a hotel and store at Pelican Waterhole, on the Western River. Floods in 1876 obliged him to shift to a more permanent spot, 2 km away at what is now Winton. Winton is the least colourful name attaching to any town in western Queensland. This is Allen's doing, as another early settler explains, in a description of the semi-official post office Allen set up. 'There was no date stamp supplied to the office, but by writing "Pelican Water-holes" and the date across the stamps, the postmark was made and the stamps were cancelled. This was found to be very slow and unsatisfactory. Allen was asked to propose a name, and he suggested that the post office should be called "Winton".'

So the town name is a time-saving device copying the name of the suburb Allen came from in England. This story is told by William Corfield in his book *Reminiscences of Queensland: 1862–1899* (p. 80). Corfield was a trader who set up in Winton in 1878, at a time when big sheep runs were being established all around—such as at nearby Vindex, Elderslie to the west and Dagworth away to the north-west, on the upper Diamantina.

The great stimulus for Winton's growth, the feature that made it the sole urban centre of a district 300 km across, was its fine array of pubs. Corfield's greatest service to the district was to establish, in 1879, the North Gregory Hotel, the biggest and most respectable pub beyond Longreach—the institution that put the town on the map, its fabled amenities and refreshments luring visitors from faraway places.

After selling the hotel, Corfield stayed on as Winton's leading merchant until in 1888 he went into Parliament, serving as the local member till 1899.

Four pubs were prospering by 1882, when the first clergyman reached Winton. He conducted some services in existing buildings, but a church was not found necessary until 1890.

Around 1880 the district appears to have been visited by a native of the Gold Coast. He was not from the Gold Coast near Brisbane, where you retire or go for a beach holiday, but from the country in Africa now known as Ghana. Early in the century, as a boy, he had joined the Dutch man o' war that was taking Prince Henry on a round-the-world trip. Calling at one country after another, it was the ideal start for a young African bent on seeing the world. He was quite a celebrity in Iceland, where no one had seen a black man before. Decades later he came to outback Queensland to work as a cook on the sheep stations. No doubt if we knew other details of his life, they would be more interesting than his name, John Smith.

In February 1883 Smith turned his back on the Waltzing Matilda district, and rode south towards Coopers Creek. Near the Thomson River, he overtook a man walking all alone with his swag. This turned out to be George Morrison, known to posterity as Chinese Morrison.

Morrison was tall, young and handsome with the fair complexion that comes from Scottish ancestors. Banjo Paterson, who wrote the words to 'Waltzing Matilda', would later describe him as 'powerful and wiry, with a strong imposing presence'. Morrison described Smith as a 'toothless darkie' and an 'old gentleman'. The two could hardly have looked more different, but on the track they struck up the rapport of kindred spirits. It was a striking coincidence that they should meet on a deserted track between pioneer sheep runs, in an area still blank on most maps.

But looked at another way, it was a natural effect of their shared attitude to the world, as a place to be traversed at will, where all obstacles look small.

At twenty, Morrison was an experienced bushman. Finishing school in 1879, he had set out alone with camping gear, from Geelong. Forty-six days later he turned up in Adelaide after a 1200 km bushwalk.

The following year, in Christmas holidays from university, he paddled 2,000 km down the Murray River to Lake Alexandrina. In 1882 he signed on a blackbirding vessel to see the pillaging of Pacific islands, to supply Kanakas to labour in the Queensland canefields. His reports on that journey for the *Age* were the foundation of his journalistic career. He continued his sea travels in steamers and on a Chinese junk, visiting New Guinea, Cooktown, Thursday Island and, finally, Normanton.

Normanton was a new town, close to the point where Burke and Wills, and then McKinlay, had given up the quest to reach the nearby Gulf of Carpentaria.

From Normanton in November 1882, Morrison set out to walk to Melbourne, with only the gear he could shoulder, and no more food than his tucker bag would hold. He was good enough with a rifle to expect to feed himself off the land, but he decided instead to travel without firearms, trusting providence and the opportunity of buying rations at the few stations along his route.

He went via Cloncurry. Then he crossed the McKinley Hills without food, in temperatures so high that the water evaporated from his water bag and he had very little to drink. He passed through Dagworth, walking along the Diamantina. Leaving the river after 180 km, he travelled across to Elderslie station near Winton. Heading south-east via a series of sheep runs, he had reached and crossed the Thomson River, shortly before John Smith encountered him.

Morrison was one of the first to cross the district on foot, and obviously he was no ordinary swaggy. He is certainly not the swagman people began to sing about twelve years later, but he is the first and last swagman to camp by the billabongs of the Diamantina who is known to have been jolly.

Thousands of others equipped just like him would trudge the same tracks in the coming years, but not for the joy of it. Morrison's descriptions in the *Age* of the experience and the country were the general reading public's first introduction to the birthplace of 'Waltzing Matilda'.

The two men continued southward together. In the *Age*, Morrison remembered his new companion as 'one of the kindest most considerate men'.

> He would stint himself of water if the day
> were hot that I might have the more. And
> this is how we fell out. We had to go one day
> 25 miles carrying water. Though parched
> with thirst he would not take his share. Not
> to be outdone I also refused any water, and
> being annoyed I vowed we must part.

Humping a swag across Australia was a small thing to Morrison. Back in Geelong by April 1883, he launched a long and ultimately successful campaign to have the vicious Kanaka trade closed down. In 1884 he travelled to Edinburgh in transports of agony, for the surgical removal of a spear tip which had broken off between his stomach and buttocks during an attempt to cross New Guinea. He stayed to complete a medical degree, then worked as a doctor in Morocco.

In 1895, while Banjo Paterson was writing 'Waltzing Matilda' by the Diamantina, Morrison was at sea, writing the witty and informative travel classic, *An Australian in China*, which no one can read without laughing out loud. In the meantime he had walked clear across China and Burma, from the Pacific to the Indian Ocean, dressed as a 'Chinaman'.

Next the *Times* appointed him its correspondent in Peking [Beijing], where, during the Boxer uprising, he helped organise the successful armed defence of the foreign community. From 1912 to his death in 1920 he was a senior adviser to the new Chinese Republic.

Politics played a big part in the history of the Waltzing Matilda district. In pioneer times, it attracted and produced politicians and their families, such as the Corfields. When Morrison was passing through, a son of Hugh Childers, Britain's Chancellor of the Exchequer, was sinking dams at Elderslie, and Prime Minister Gladstone's nephew was droving a mob of cattle to the Northern Territory.

Other stations near Winton were part-owned by Sir Thomas McIlwraith, Premier of Queensland for many years in the 1880s and 1890s.

One group of people powerfully attracted to inland Queensland in the nineteenth century were squatter families from Victoria. In the 1830s and onwards, these families had established large pastoral stations in Victoria, on land leased from the Crown. But Land Acts in the 1860s entitled small-scale farmers to take up the same land, and the squatters found themselves being crowded out as Victoria became closely settled. Heading for new opportunities, the squatters overlanded their livestock clear across New South Wales to take up vast runs in Queensland.

Famously opulent Victorian families, such as the Chirnsides, the Fairbairns, the Armytages and the Manifolds, became established around places such as Longreach, Winton and Hughenden. With their ample capital they could afford to add Queensland stations to their reduced runs in Victoria, and to finance the new operations from their old fortunes.

On a lower tier economically were families who had to give up on Victoria and transplant all their pastoral operations to have the means to establish themselves in outback Queensland. The Macphersons—who took over Dagworth station on the Diamantina—came from this bracket. They sank their limited wealth into Dagworth and borrowed heavily from the bank against the huge revenues their wool clip would bring.

UP CAME THE SQUATTERS

THE NAMES OF STATIONS BEYOND WINTON reveal something about the type of people who founded them. Although some are local, like Kynuna (pronounced Ky-new-na) and Oondooroo, many names recall the old countries where squatter families originated—Ayrshire Downs and Llan-rheidol for instance. Some Aboriginal names are not native, including Warnambool and Quambetook: Victorian names, stirring fond memories of a more recent old country.

People remark that Dagworth was a perverse name to give a sheep station, though in time it would prove accurate enough. Dagworth was a horse that apparently ran a third in the Melbourne Cup. But he is only remembered for lending his name to the station, founded in 1876 and bought by the Macphersons in the 1880s, where Australia's favourite song was born. Racehorses were the preferred hobby of station families, and just as Dagworth gave his name to a station in Queensland, The Banjo gave his to a poet from a station in New South Wales.

In Australia the first settlers in grazing country were usually squatters and the people who worked for them. They leased large runs from colonial governments, on the understanding that they might later be resumed. In the earliest phase of settlement it meant there were two societies of white people in bush areas.

Station people from the manager down to the youngest boundary rider lived and worked on the station year round.

The itinerants humped their swags out to the stations when work was offering; shearing employed larger numbers than any other seasonal activity. Other itinerants included carriers and drovers. They all tended to be based in the towns or to have small properties in closer settled districts. They looked on the stations further out as a source of revenue and support without caring much about those who lived on them. A lot of the station people seem to have thought of the itinerants as a necessary evil rather than as part of their authentic bush community.

In the next stage of development, colonial governments promoted more intensive farming and increased the permanent rural population, by encouraging people of very modest means to take up small blocks on favourable terms, as independent farmers. The blocks were called selections, and they were usually carved out of the leaseholds of the squatters, who resented the selectors for dismembering their stations.

The itinerants didn't care much for selectors either. Also known as cockies, selectors were notoriously hard up and stingy; they were hard taskmasters and would sooner work themselves and their families into the ground than employ one more swagman than they could avoid.

From the 1860s onwards the squatters and swaggies began to find some affinity in a shared lament for the old bush ways. Victorian writer Joseph Furphy (1843–1912) explained it in 'The Gumsucker's Dirge':

> For the settlements extend till they seem to
>   have no end;
> Spreading silently, you can't tell when or
>   how;
> And a home-infested land stretches out on
>   every hand,
> So there is no Up the Country for us now.

On the six-foot mountain peak, up and
  down the dubious creek,
Where the cockatoos alone should make a
  row,
There the rooster tears his throat, to
  announce with homely note,
That there is no Up the Country for us now.

Where the dingo should be seen, sounds the
  Army tambourine,
While the hardest case surrenders with a
  vow;
And the church-bell, going strong, makes us
  feel we've lived too long,
Since there is no Up the Country for us now.

And along the pine-ridge side, where the
  mallee-hen should hide,
You will see some children driving home a
  cow;
Whilst, ballooning on a line, female garniture
  gives sign,
That there is no Up the Country for us now.

Here, in place of emu's eggs, you will find
  surveyors' pegs,
And the culvert where there ought to be a
  slough;

There, a mortise in the ground, shows the
	digger has been round,
And has left no Up the Country for us now.

Across this fenced-in view, like our friend the
	well-sung Jew,
Goes the swaggy, with a frown upon his
	brow,
He is cabin'd, cribb'd, confin'd, for the
	thought is on his mind,
That there is no Up the Country for him
	now.

And the boy that bolts from home has no
	decent place to roam,
No region with adventure to endow,
But his ardent spirit cools at the sight of
	farms and schools,
Hence, there is no Up the Country for him
	now.

Queensland, where the government was encouraging a first wave of settlement by leasing vast inland grazing runs, became the promised land of the bushmen. Squatters indulged their liberality and grand visions without fear of being closed in. In the 1930s, Banjo Paterson looked back on it in a radio talk:

Longreach and Winton, which nowadays are
cities of the plains, were four-in-hand towns
in those days. The districts around
Longreach and Winton were inhabited by
squatter kings who made royal progresses to
each other's stations, driving four horses in
harness with four spare horses, driven loose
by a black boy, following up to be used as a
change halfway through the journey.

There was a lot of Melbourne money in
those parts. Chirnside and Riley were at
Vindex, Knox at Eversham, the Ramsays at
Oondooroo, Bells, Fairbairns, *et hoc genus
omne* at other places.

Vol. II, p. 498

The disappearance of so much Melbourne
money into the black hole of outback Queensland
no doubt contributed to the dramatic collapse of
the economy of Victoria in the 1890s depression.

In 1895 Banjo was the guest of the Macphersons
at Dagworth when he wrote 'Waltzing Matilda' and
he must have had Christina's brother Bob Macpherson in mind when he introduced 'the squatter
mounted on his thoroughbred'. He also had him in
mind when he wrote of 'the magnate "out back"
who shears 150,000 sheep and has an overdraft like
the National Debt' (vol. I, p. 362). Bob had shared

statistics with him, including the melancholy revelation that they owed more than £100,000—probably over $20 million at today's values.

Banjo, who'd been raised on a mountain station in the high country behind Yass, was an admirer of station life, and admired the way it was pursued in Queensland. In *The Cook's Dog* (1919) one of his characters was a young girl from Scotland who thought back fondly on childhood years in Queensland:

> With the optimism of youth she had taken it
> for granted that her cousin had been the
> same as the other squatters she had known
> in Queensland—important men in their own
> districts, looked up to by everybody . . . She
> had expected to find things rough after
> Scotland, but the roughness would be made
> up for by the careless profusion, the
> contempt for trifles, the freedom and the
> fullness of the life that she remembered in
> the old days.
>
> Vol. II, p. 404

Even the socialistic writers of those times and the underpaid workers had a sort of grudging admiration for the squatter: for the dashing figure he cut and the huge risks he took to open new country. The typical squatter family made little demonstrations of opulence, and went to the best schools; visiting town they stayed at exclusive clubs and their manners were fine for Government House—but in their lives and work they had to cope with tough and hazardous conditions, and plenty went stoically to their ruin on the back of a change in fortune. One of Banjo's outback trips in the 1890s was with a would-be selector: 'a young Victorian who meant to take up country on Oondooroo'.

In a very straightforward way he went and told Mr M. F. Ramsay of his intention. The Ramsays had come out with a great deal of capital and one of them had bowled for the Gentlemen of England, so the young fellow got a friendly reception.

'It's alright, young fellow,' said Ramsay, 'don't worry about taking a bit of our country. We've been very nearly broke three times on this place and if you can show us how to make money off 1000 acres while we can't make it off a million, we'll give you a good salary to manage Oondooroo for the rest of your life.'

Vol. II, p. 499

'Waltzing Matilda' was written by someone who sympathised with swaggies who were down on their luck. Many people think of it as a plea for the battler who faces life without wealth or privilege. But before concluding that the squatter is the villain of the little drama, it's worth remembering that Banjo not only got on well with such people but often had to feel sorry for them, as he did during the shocking drought of 1901:

> Away out on the Diamantina and
> neighbouring districts, the 'squatters' have
> lost all their stock and most of their money
> trying to make something of those
> 'undeveloped resources'. We talk about our
> 'glorious country' and all that sort of thing
> but a few years in Northern Queensland
> make one doubt whether it is so glorious
> after all.
>
> *Sydney Morning Herald*, 9 November 1901;
> vol. II, p. 16

THE COMPOSER
AND THE POET

THE MACPHERSONS, WHO HAD COME from Scotland in 1854, set up as graziers in northern Victoria. In 1865 their homestead was visited by Mad Dan Morgan, vilest bushranger of his times. Morgan's exploits were dashing and daring, but he wasn't one of those engaging bushrangers who inspire respect and public sympathy. He was mad, murderous, vicious and vindictive, and nobody much liked him. Morgan ordered Ewan Macpherson, his wife and older children into the dining room and got them to provide dinner, drinks, supper and music before putting him up for the night.

After dinner, he excused the nursemaid, Alice Macdonald, so she could see to the baby crying in another room. This crying was done by the Macpherson's new daughter Christina, who thereby gave Alice an opportunity to rush to a neighbouring house with news of the crisis. As Mad Dan snoozed away peacefully, forty police, summoned in the night by the neighbour, gathered around the homestead, to wait for his morning appearance. But they never made an arrest. While Ewan Macpherson showed Mad Dan to the stables for a getaway horse, the bushranger caught a fatal bullet in the back, fired by the Macphersons' stockman, John Quinlan.

Little Christina, who had cried for Australia at the critical moment, was followed by another daughter, Margaret. Christina, like her siblings and so many respectable offspring of pastoral families, went to school in Melbourne. In 1891 Margaret married Stewart McArthur. Their daughter, Christina's niece, later wrote that her Aunt Chris was a frequent visitor to their family property, Meningoort, near Camperdown in the Western District of Victoria.

It must have been on such a visit in April 1894 that Chris went with the McArthurs to the annual races at Warrnambool. Facing the Southern Ocean, by the mouth of the Hopkins River, Warrnambool is the closest major town to Meningoort, and its annual racing carnival has always drawn spectators from the country around. For the well-heeled and influential pastoral families of western Victoria, it was a great social occasion. Over three days in 1894 the crowds were entertained by the 'town band', properly known as the Garrison Artillery Band.

Chris Macpherson had an ear for music and family members recalled that she used to remember tunes and hum and play them later. They were probably right, but she also had a creative streak, and one of the tunes played at Warrnambool in 1894 emerged from her memory into something different—something a lot of people would be humming and playing before long. By her own account it was that tune played by the band at the races that gave her the music for 'Waltzing Matilda'.

In December that year her mother died, and Ewan Macpherson decided to leave Melbourne with his girls Chris and Jean, to join their brothers at Dagworth. Then, as now, it would be hard to find a more radical change of scene without going overseas. Their city was the largest in Australia and one of the most imposingly built in the world; lavishly it paraded the achievements, ornaments and ailments of civilisation. Its glittering shops, vast pleasure gardens, tramways, pavements, and ornate palaces of brick and stone had no counterparts in all of Queensland, let alone in the remote destination of the Macphersons. The infrequent buildings there were of wood and corrugated iron; sometimes their frameworks were unfinished boughs. Even the fabulous North Gregory Hotel would have looked humble and rustic on a Melbourne street.

It's possible the Macpherson ladies missed the Melbourne sights more than Melbourne society; not just because Melbourne hadn't produced husbands to go with their good looks and upbringing—but also because the district they went to was home to other people like them, even some who had moved in the same circles in Victoria. Undaunted by big distances, the Macphersons and their neighbours often visited Winton and each other's stations.

There were the Rileys, who had bought into Vindex station with the Chirnsides in the 1880s. Fred Riley was living in town with his wife Marie at their house, Aloha, on Vindex Street. They ran various businesses including the Post Office Hotel, across the street from where the Waltzing Matilda Centre is now. In 1895 Fred's sister Sarah visited and stayed at Aloha and Vindex station. She was an old friend of Christina's from school, and it was natural to invite her out to Dagworth.

Sarah had been engaged for eight years. Her fiancé, 'Bartie', was not one of the Melbourne set. He had been raised on stations in New South Wales, but by his own account he had taken to working in Sydney, in a dingy little office.

Andrew Barton Paterson (1864–1941) had his office in Sydney, at the Bond Street premises of Street and Paterson, the law firm in which he practised as a partner. Born at Narambla in the central west of New South Wales, he'd lived and worked on family properties, but been sent to Sydney Grammar for secondary schooling. He began in 1885 sending poems to the *Bulletin* under his nom de plume, 'The Banjo', a horse's name.

Horses were his special love, and one of those first poems in the *Bulletin*, published on 10 October 1886, was 'A Dream of the Melbourne Cup'. 'The Man from Snowy River', written in 1890 is more famous, of course—one of the shortest works of literature ever made into a movie. That too is a horse poem, but its active ingredient is the underdog hero, the outsider who takes centre stage—a familiar figure in Paterson's writing, and a favourite feature of Australian culture from those days till these:

> And one was there, a stripling on a small
>   and weedy beast,
> He was something like a racehorse under-
>   sized,
> With a touch of Timor pony—three parts
>   thoroughbred at least—
> And such as are by mountain horsemen prized.

He was hard and tough and wiry—just the
    sort that won't say die—
There was courage in his quick impatient
    tread;
And he bore the badge of gameness in his
    bright and fiery eye,
And the proud and lofty carriage of his head.

But still so slight and weedy one would
    doubt his power to stay,
And the old man said, 'That horse will never
    do
For a long and tiring gallop—lad, you'd
    better stop away,
Those hills are far too rough for such as you.'

Vol. I, p. 112

In the vintage style of Paterson, the details all concern the horse, but with that he secures every reader's feelings for the man.

Trading on the triumph of the marginal competitor in 'The Man from Snowy River', and the tragedies of other underdogs in other works, Paterson was tapping into a current already present in the Australian character, which he helped to foster and protect forever.

By the time he wrote 'The Man from Snowy River', Banjo was already a big name in poetry, mainly because of 'Clancy of the Overflow', published in 1889, and the raptures and opposition it called up. It tells the true story of a small matter Paterson dealt with in his legal practice: a man he wrote to about an unpaid debt.

CLANCY OF THE OVERFLOW

I had written him a letter which I had, for want of better
Knowledge, sent to where I met him down the Lachlan,
   years ago,
He was shearing when I knew him, so I sent the letter to
   him
Just 'on spec', addressed as follows: 'Clancy, of the
   Overflow'.

And an answer came directed in a writing unexpected,
(And I think the same was written with a thumbnail
   dipped in tar)
'Twas his shearing mate who wrote it, and *verbatim* I
   will quote it:
Clancy's gone to Queensland droving, and we don't
   know where he are.'

In my wild erratic fancy visions come to me of Clancy
Gone a-droving 'down the Cooper' where the western
   drovers go;
As the stock are slowly stringing, Clancy rides behind
   them singing,
For the drover's life has pleasures that the townsfolk
   never know.

And the bush hath friends to meet him, and their kindly
    voices greet him
In the murmur of the breezes and the river on its bars,
And he sees the vision splendid of the sunlit plains
    extended,
And at night the wondrous glory of the everlasting
    stars.

I am sitting in my dingy little office, where a stingy
Ray of sunlight struggles feebly down between the houses
    tall,
And the foetid air and gritty of the dusty, dirty city
Through the open window floating, spreads its foulness
    over all.

And in place of lowing cattle, I can hear the fiendish rattle
Of the tramways and the buses making hurry down the
    street,
And the language uninviting of the gutter children fighting,
Comes fitfully and faintly through the ceaseless tramp of
    feet.

And the hurrying people daunt me, and their pallid faces
    haunt me
As they shoulder one another in their rush and nervous
    haste,
With their eager eyes and greedy, and their stunted forms
    and weedy,
For townsfolk have no time to grow, they have no time
    to waste.

And I somehow rather fancy that I'd like to change with
    Clancy,

Like to take a turn at droving where the seasons come
  and go,
While he faced the round eternal of the cashbook and the
  journal—
But I doubt he'd suit the office, Clancy, of 'The
  Overflow'.

Vol. I, p. 125

This is a heartfelt demonstration of Paterson's admiration of bush life, western Queensland's romantic call on him, and specific enthusiasms such as riding and song. But 'Clancy' turned out to be one of Australia's most controversial poems. Banjo's truthfulness was challenged; his critics protested that in the safe comfort of his city office, he glorified a life of hardship and pretended that a punishing environment was genial.

Edward Dyson's poem 'The Fact of the Matter' appeared in the *Bulletin* of 30 July 1892:

...
I'm wondering why those fellers who go
  building chipper ditties
'Bout the rosy times out droving and the dust
  and dirt of cities,
Don't sling the bloomin' office, strike some
  drover for a billet

And soak up all the glory that comes handy
    while they fill it.

On 27 August 1892 Francis Kenna wrote 'Banjo of the Overflow' in a similar vein, and on 20 August 1892 'The Overflow of Clancy' by 'H.H.C.C.' drew the poet's attention to attractions that might be keeping him in Sydney:

And the pub hath friends to greet him and
    between the acts they treat him
While he's swapping 'fairy twisters' with the
    girls behind their bars.
And he sees a vista splendid when the ballet
    is extended
And at night he's in his glory with the comic
    opera stars.

The best-known exchange in the wake of Clancy was the 'Town versus Bush' poetic debate of 1892. Henry Lawson (1867–1922) and Banjo tackled each other in verse, month after month in the *Bulletin,* over whether the bush was better or the city. Life was a hard battle to Lawson who, unlike Paterson, had never been comfortably off; Lawson associated the bush with deprivation and sympathised with downtrodden people he felt were stuck there. So they both meant what they said in the argument, but they kept the debate going as long as they could, because they wanted the money and the exposure. When they ran out of things to say, Paterson concluded, on 1 October 1892:

> But that ends it, Mister Lawson, and it's time
>   to say goodbye…
> And if fortune only favours us we will take
>   the road some day,
> And go droving down the river 'neath the
>   sunshine and the stars
> And then we'll come to Sydney and
>   vermilionize the bars.

Vol. I, p. 176

('Vermilionize the bars' is another way to say 'paint the town red'.)

The *Bulletin*, where these dialogues went on, wasn't just a paper—it was a unique institution. It gave writers such as Dyson, Lawson and Paterson a high profile throughout Australia. It was the central seedbed for the most vibrant flowering of Australian literature.

This was thanks to the vision and practicality of its co-founder and editor, J. F. Archibald (1856–1919). His name lives on in his bequests, including the Archibald Prize, Australia's leading art award. The Archibald Fountain, in Sydney's Hyde

Park, the finest of fountains, is another. There used to be a plaque beside it explaining the significance of the huge bronze statues, drawn from Greek myth, which represent the various accomplishments of life. Some bureaucratic vandal has had this replaced with a new plaque that quotes twaddle from his filing cabinet. The old plaque pointed out that the top statue represents Apollo, god of light, inspiring his world to culture and knowledge.

If you are a sculptor, you could put Archibald himself up in bronze on a pedestal like that, his arm stretched out like Apollo's—and render only justice to what Archibald does for the mind and spirit of his countrymen. Many years after writing 'Waltzing Matilda' Paterson looked back at Archibald's achievement: 'When his name is forgotten and people ask, "who was this Archibald who left this bequest?", the question can be answered by saying, "He was the first man who believed in the home-made Australian article"'.

Archibald made his way into journalism as a teenager in Warrnambool, on the *Examiner* and as one of the founding staff of the *Warrnambool Standard*. He moved on to Melbourne, the Palmer River goldfield in Cape York and then Sydney, where he started the *Bulletin* in 1880.

He envisaged Australia as a cultural centre in its own right, and he could not bear to see it as a

colonial outpost of British civilisation. His readers
were to be Australians, not displaced Europeans,
and he was determined to give them stuff that valued
their own experience, thoughts and aspirations.

'It is hard at this date to convey the almost eso-
teric reverence with which Archie and the *Bulletin*
were regarded in those days,' writes Norman Lindsay in *Bohemians at the Bulletin*.

> The *Bulletin* initiated an amazed recognition
> that Australia was 'home', and that was the
> anvil on which Archibald hammered out the
> rough substance of the national ego. (p. 5)

Archibald's most effective method was to discover and encourage people who executed his vision
in poetry, prose and art. In 1900 Lindsay was one,
especially in the capacity of *Bulletin* cartoonist.

Paterson was one of the first, when Archibald
picked him out from the thousands who submitted
poems in the 1880s. When Archibald wrote to him
it was almost as if he could sense 'Waltzing
Matilda' in there somewhere:

> I want you to remember that Australia is a
> big place and I want you to write the stuff
> that will appeal not only to Sydney people
> but that will be of interest to the pearler up

on Thursday Island and the farmer down in Victoria...In all public issues the press are apt to sing in chorus. If you go to a concert you may hear a man sing in discord which is put there by the composer, and that discord catches the ear over the voices of the chorus. Well don't be afraid to sing the discord...for the same reason do not be afraid to cheer for the underdog...

Another champion of Australian writing in Sydney was the bookseller and publisher, George Robertson, founder of Angus and Robertson. Late in 1895 he published the first book of Paterson's work, *The Man from Snowy River and other Verses*. Suddenly Paterson—who'd only been known to *Bulletin* readers as 'The Banjo'—became a national celebrity with a name.

The first print run sold out in a fortnight, and the 10,000 copies purchased within the first year were a small fraction of the total eventually sold, mainly in a country with a small population but many poetry lovers.

Banjo thus became one of the most popular poets in the English language; second only to the Indian-born English writer, Rudyard Kipling (1865–1936). The two men relished and influenced each other's work. However they are easy to distinguish and it seems curious that Paterson has been described as derivative of Kipling. When Kipling got his copy of Banjo's book in 1895, he wrote to Angus and Robertson:

> There can't be too many men in this world
> singing about what they know and love and
> want other people to know and love. There
> may be, as you hint, a little Kipling in some
> of the lines, but, for that matter we all steal
> from each other (it's part of our business),
> and he'll find his own stride quite soon
> enough.
>
> 10 December 1895

They became good friends a few years later during the Boer War in South Africa, where Banjo discovered first hand what a one-eyed British imperialist Kipling was. While politically their outlooks were awry, poetically they were close and each had similar aspirations for his art. In a broad way, they were writing the same kind of poetry.

Professional critics and professors of literature, from those days till now, disdain Paterson's work, seeing him as something less than a poet: a mere versifier whose writings are only worth keeping as examples of the milieu they come from. Paterson mounted no direct defence, but he developed a poetical theory. He rules himself out with conventional modesty: 'this only applies to real poetry, not to the verse that most of us write'. Real poetry is 'very rare and very wonderful...One might almost think that true poetry is the work of some disembodied spirit'.

Yet when Paterson asks whether Kipling's work is poetry or mere verse, and applies his personal poetic theory to the test, it is clear enough that his own poetry can be rated in the same way. At one point he even takes 'The Man from Snowy River' as an example.

Poetry to him is instinct in human beings, 'older than civilisation, possibly older than speech'. The poetry which succeeds that primaeval form is 'tribal poetry'—a concept inspired by his experiences at corroborees in the Northern Territory and among Torres Strait islander pearling crews. Basic poetry moves the members of tribes together. Paterson traces the evolution of tribal poetry into narrative poetry of fact, then of fiction. Ultimately came 'poems of fancy: poems about emotion: poems about moonlight and beautiful women: poems about life, and love and liquor'.

In the tribal context, he observes, a poet may be making up a story or a state of mind in which he has not actually taken part—but it is true poetry, if the listener feels the truth of it. Thus poetry advanced to its full maturity in prehistoric times. Tribal poetry and true poetry are the same thing for him.

When he says Kipling is 'a true tribal poet', we should understand that Banjo himself is 'true' and 'tribal' whenever his work rings true deeply with those who hear it. Many of his poems obviously fit into the intermediate story-telling phase of evolution; but some of his work, including 'Waltzing Matilda', belongs to the ultimate phase of tribal development.

Of course sophisticated critics and literature professors are protected from this idea by their disdain for Paterson. But insofar as their judgement that Banjo, and others like him, are not poets is born of myopic ignorance, we can safely disregard it; it is only worth noticing as an example of their methods and the value of their work.

Country New South Wales is the setting for most of the poems in *The Man from Snowy River and other Verses*, but Banjo's penchant for western Queensland emerges in places where extreme remoteness is part of the story:

> On the outer Barcoo, where the churches are
>   few
> And the men of religion are scanty
> On a road never crossed 'cept by folk that
>   are lost,
> One Michael Magee had a shanty.
>
> Vol. I, p. 202

is a popular example, from 'A Bush Christening'.

While working on this book, Paterson left Sydney for Queensland, and the first of several trips that took him to the Winton area, presumably at the suggestion of his fiancée, Sarah Riley. One can imagine his eagerness at the prospect of visiting the newly founded townships and the big outback stations.

From Brisbane to Rockhampton he went by sea, before they built the railway along the coast. It was a comfortable, relaxing way to see sub-tropical islands and coastlines, ending in a river journey up to the heart of the city.

At Rockhampton railway station, he found a train of goods wagons, with some passenger carriages at the end, and joined it for the journey along the newly finished Central Railway. Allowing for the legendary slowness of Queensland trains, the 680 km trip would have taken longer than 24 hours, with lengthy stops to handle goods along the way. Perhaps some passengers envied Banjo's experience with horses: no doubt he was able to keep his seat as the train bucked along the cheaply laid rails of the pioneer line. The lurching carriages were quite well furnished, there were plenty of breaks for refreshments, and the ever-changing shapes and colours of the country out the window would have made a pleasant journey for a curious observer.

Heading west, parallel with the Tropic of Capricorn, the train took him quickly across the narrow coastal plain, then laboured over eastern slopes of the Great Dividing Range to the farming land round Emerald. West of that it wound its way through the arid and spectacular Drummond Ranges, the wheel flanges singing against the rails as the locomotive took the tightest bends.

After that they were into the open grazing country of the inland, where good grazing land alternates with stretches of soil too poor to support pastures. The terminus was Longreach. Connecting coaches on to Winton were run by Cobb and Co.—a name W. H. Corfield, in his book *Reminiscences of Queensland 1986–1899*, rightly described as 'a synonym for efficiency and punctuality' (p. 84). Cobb and Co. had the best drivers and coaches, but after a day on rough dusty or muddy bush roads, most passengers were relieved to arrive and glad to get off. Coaches were usually piled high with luggage, parcels and mail. The dearest seats were inside, out on top was cheap, but enthusiasts like Banjo probably preferred the box seat at the front near the driver. A full coach was a cramped vehicle and every passenger arriving in Winton would have been in immediate need of a stretch, a wash and a lie down, after lurching 180 km across the plain.

The final stage of Banjo's journey to the Diamantina would have been a more relaxed and genial affair, with the engaging company of Sarah and the Macphersons, aboard the Dagworth buggy, and no gruelling timetable to stick to. In his novel *An Outback Marriage* some of Banjo's characters make a Queensland trip of the same sort, giving us an idea of what it would have been like for him:

> After a short sea journey, they took train to a dusty backblocks township, where Gordon picked up one of the many outfits which he had scattered over the country, and which in this case consisted of a vehicle, a dozen or so of horses, and a black boy named Frying Pan.
>
> They drove four horses in a low, American-made buggy, and travelled about

fifty miles a day. Frying Pan was invaluable.
He seemed to have a natural affinity for
horses…

At night they usually managed to reach a
station, where the man in charge would greet
them effusively, and beg them to turn their
horses out and stay a week—or a year—or
two…

XVI, vol. I, p. 400

The most likely series of events is that Sarah
Riley introduced her fiancé to the Macphersons in
Winton, and they both took up the invitation to
stay a while at Dagworth. They made the trip in a
good season, when the soil was moist, the grass was
green and the sheep were fat.

The first day's travel from Winton would have
taken them to Ayrshire Downs station, where they
stayed the night as guests of the Morrisons, who
were friends of the Rileys and Macphersons. The
next day in the buggy would bring them to Dagworth in time for the evening meal.

Banjo would have had the opportunity to take
a bath, don a fresh shirt, jacket and tie, and join the
others for a good dinner and genteel conversation,
before ending his trip from Sydney in a comfortable
bed.

SWAGMEN

A VISIT TO DAGWORTH WAS A DIFFERENT proposition for a swagman—one of hundreds travelling up the Diamantina each year. A swag unrolled on the hard ground was his bed—under the stars, or in some hopeful arrangement of oilcloth, netting or canvas, intended to keep out loud choruses of mozzies.

Our swaggy, if he had no horse or bike, would have taken lifts when the chance came along; the coach fare was usually too dear for him, and he went many miles on foot, humping all his meagre luggage from one campsite to the next.

The pockets of his worn clothes were stuffed with bits and pieces—string, papers, rags, matches and so on—but not with money. The depression of the 1890s imposed financial constraints on rural workers: shortages of work, downwards pressure on wages and strikes. But even in the best of times swagmen did not take to the track because their financial condition enabled them to choose it as an attractive option. The best paid work—shearing above all—was limited to short seasons, leaving many to face long spells unpaid. And the habits of the swagman did not make for financial wellbeing: he resented having to seek work at all if he still had any money, and when he was paid, his main objective was to spend quickly. The second most popular bush song explains the process of knocking down a cheque, in its closing verses:

CLICK GO THE SHEARS

Out on the board the old shearer stands,
Grasping his shears in his long, bony hands,
Fixed is his gaze on a bare bellied joe,
Glory if he gets her, won't he make the ringer go.

Chorus Click go the shears boys, click, click, click.
Wide is his blow and his hand moves quick,
The ringer looks around and he's beaten by a blow,
And he curses the old snagger with the blue bellied joe.

In the middle of the floor in his cane-bottomed chair
Is the boss of the boards, with eyes everywhere;
Notes well each fleece as it come to the screen,
Paying strict attention if it's taken off clean.

The tar-boy is there, a-waiting in demand,
With his blackened tar-pot, and his tarry hand;
Sees one old sheep with a cut upon its back,
Hears what he's waiting for, 'Tar here, Jack!'

Shearing is all over and we've all got our cheques,
Roll up your swag for we're off on the tracks;
The first pub we come to, it's there we'll have a spree,
And everyone that comes along it's, 'Come and drink
    with me.'

Down by the bar the old shearer stands,
Grasping his glass in his lean bony hands;
Fixed is his gaze on a green painted keg,
Glory, he'll get down on her, ere he stirs a peg.

There we leave him standing, shouting for all hands,
Whilst all around him every shouter stands;
His eyes are on the cask, which now is lowering fast,
He works hard and he drinks hard, and he goes to hell
    at last.

When financial conditions were dire, a man
could survive by humping his swag, and taking to
the track. It was called 'going on the wallaby'. He
didn't in fact have to dine on wallaby. It was a con-
vention in the backblocks that a swagman calling
on a station must be given rations of flour, meat,
sugar and tea. In theory this was because he had
come to work, but a true member of the wallaby
brigade timed his arrival for sundown, when it was

too late to start work till the next day. He was often gone first thing in the morning, just as the station manager would have feared. Surviving on rations was getting tougher though, as squatters moved out into more remote areas, where the distances between homesteads were great. Swagmen took to other measures as Chris Macpherson herself explained, in a letter she wrote to Thomas Wood in the 1930s, but never posted: 'There are always a number of men travelling about the country, some riding and some on foot, they are usually given rations at the various stations that they come to, but in Queensland the distances are so great that they help themselves without asking.'

In his 1905 book, *Old Bush Songs*, Paterson included an anonymous song:

THE WALLABY BRIGADE

You often have been told of regiments brave and bold,
But we are the bravest in the land;
We're called the Tag-rag Band, and we rally in
    Queensland,
We are members of the Wallaby Brigade.

Chorus Tramp, tramp, tramp across the borders,
      The swagmen are rolling up, I see.
      When the shearing's at an end we'll go fishing in
        a bend.
      Then hurrah! for the Wallaby Brigade.

When you are leaving camp, you must ask some brother
    tramp
If there are any jobs to be had,
Or what sort of a shop that station is to stop
For a member of the Wallaby Brigade.

You ask if they want men, you ask for rations then—
If they don't stump up a warning should be made;
To teach them better sense—why, 'Set fire to their fence'
Is the war cry of the Wallaby Brigade.

The squatters thought us done when they fenced in all
    their run,
But a prettier mistake they never made;
You've only to sport your dover and knock a monkey
    over—
There's cheap mutton for the Wallaby Brigade.

Now when the shearing's in, our harvest will begin,
Our swags for a spell down will be laid;
But when our cheques are drank we will join the Tag-rag
    rank,
Limeburners in the Wallaby Brigade.

'Knock a monkey over' is another way to say
'kill a jumbuck'. Monkey used to be the only synonym for sheep that was popular in the vernacular. Monkey, which was common, is forgotten now,
while jumbuck, which was rare, is known everywhere. That's all because Banjo thought jumbuck

worth conserving, but he didn't care for monkey, and it died.

There was only so much a meagrely equipped swaggy could do with the carcase of a sheep. He'd cook up the choicest cuts as an immediate solution to the problem of his hunger; he'd wrap a bit more up and cram it in an old sugar bag or whatever other calico bag he'd managed to scrounge for carrying tucker. The dismembered carcase he'd just leave where it lay, for the flies and eagles to enjoy. He could grill meat over his camp fire, bake it in the coals or boil it in the billy that he always carried for tea making and cooking.

You could get purpose-made billies cheaply, but the exemplary swagman we're talking about had saved himself that expense by adding a wire handle to a big, old jam tin, and improvising a roughly fitting lid.

His other equipment included a water bag, designed to cool the water by evaporation from its wet sides. It hung from loops with a stick threaded through, so he could keep it off his clothes and gear. He also had a quartpot—a big multi-purpose mug. On the long tracks of Queensland he didn't carry things that had only one use, except his pipe. Most of his personal items were packed in the swag, which he made by rolling up blankets in the oilcloth that served as his fly or groundsheet when camping. When travelling he carried the swag comfortably folded on his shoulder, so he always had a hand free to wave away the flies. In a thousand pictures, you see the corks dangling from his hat for this very purpose. Now hats like that are a product line in souvenir shops. Certainly the tourists have taken a lot more of them to their far-away countries than ever Australian swagmen took out along the track.

The flies were regrettable, but he didn't bother with corks to ward them off. He found a lot of things regrettable—the heat, the cold, the rain, the dust, the quality of rations, the work, the conditions and the rate of pay.

In 1891 these latter concerns got out of hand. Over fifteen hundred irate workers downed their swags in central Queensland and refused to shear on the terms being offered. Under the Eureka flag they gathered at Barcaldine (pronounced Bar-calld'n), 70 miles east of Longreach. The graziers began recruiting scab labour and tensions built as the colonial government sent more and more police. It feared a Eureka-style uprising and eventually mobilised troops, with an artillery piece (a rare object in colonial Queensland).

The unrest settled down with scarcely any violence, in what was seen as a win for the employers.

But the labour movement achieved a new prominence and organisation that made it formidable for ninety years to come. Traditionally, it was at a meeting by the railway at Barcaldine that a large group of the strikers founded the Labor Party. A tree, known as 'The Tree of Knowledge' by the railway station, where the party is said to have first convened, is an attraction ogled nowadays by many travellers—though only while the train is at the station. Like the federal Labor Party, the tree has survived some ups and downs, including a major split. While this book was being written, some vandal with no feeling for history, or far too much, doused it with 30 litres of poison. A little earlier it was showing more vigour than the federal Labor Party, but this is now in doubt.

In 1894 labour unrest brewed again, as the graziers tried to hold shearers to depressed pay rates worked out the year before. Now there emerged among the strikers a destructive group who took extreme measures. There were many cases of intimidation and violence directed against scabs. On 4 July they went to new extremes and burnt down Ayrshire Downs woolshed. Redcliffe woolshed followed on 25 July. In August, four more Queensland sheds were burnt down, including Manuka, not far from Winton. At Redcliffe, a large amount of valuable wool was destroyed also. At Eroungella a constable was tied to a tree and left till help came.

By 1 September at Dagworth station, where 'Waltzing Matilda' would shortly be invented, the Macpherson brothers and their men had driven a mob of sheep to the woolshed, so shearing by scab labour could begin on Monday the 3rd. On guard against the arsonists' depredations, about twenty people, including the Macphersons, their overseer and a policeman, were staying in huts adjacent to the shed.

During the night, an armed party of strikers crept up, determined to burn the shed down, and planning to shoot so that none of its defenders could save it. Banjo describes the episode briefly in an essay for the *Bulletin* on 18 October 1902 entitled 'The Dog':

> Dogs, like horses, have very keen intuition. They know when a man is frightened of them, and they know when the men around them are frightened, though they may not know the cause. In the great Queensland strike, when the shearers attacked Dagworth shed, some rifle volleys were exchanged, the shed was burnt, and the air was full of human electricity, each man giving out waves of fear and excitement. Mark now the effect it had on the dogs. They were not in the

fighting; nobody fired at them and nobody
spoke to them; but every dog left his master,
left the sheep, and went away about six miles
to the homestead. There wasn't a dog about
the shed next day, after the fight. They knew
there was something out of the common in
the way of danger.

Vol. II, p. 117

The two groups at the shed deliberately fired on
each other although, deliberately or accidentally, no
one was hit. While the shed was on fire, rain came
and helped put it out. However it was mostly burnt
and it was too late to save the 140 penned up lambs
that died from the fire.

The fact that no one was hurt does not mean
that this was not serious stuff. In Australian history
you can count on the fingers of one hand the gun-
fights between armed groups of more than a couple
of men. There was Eureka in 1853, the capture of
the Kelly Gang in 1880, the Milperra Massacre of
1984, some other fight surely, and the woolshed
fight at Dagworth in 1894, just before Banjo
Paterson came to visit.

THE OLD BARK HUT

Oh, my name is Bob the Swagman, before you all I stand,
I've seen a lot of ups and downs while travelling through
    the land.
I once was well to do, my boys, but now I am stumped up,
And I'm forced to go on rations in an old bark hut.

Chorus   In an old bark hut, in an old bark hut.
          I'm forced to go on rations in an old bark hut.

Ten pounds of flour, ten pounds of beef, some sugar and
    some tea,
That's all they give to a hungry man, until the Seventh Day.
If you don't be mighty sparing, you'll go with a hungry
    gut—
For that's one of the great misfortunes in an old bark hut.

The bucket you boil your beef in has to carry water, too,
And they'll say you're getting mighty flash if you should
    ask for two.
I've a billy, and a pintpot, and a broken handled cup,
And they all adorn the table in the old bark hut.

Faith, the table is not made of wood, as many you have
    seen—
For if I had one half so good, I'd think myself serene—
'Tis only an old sheet of bark—God knows when it was
    cut—
It was blown from off the rafters of the old bark hut.

And of furniture, there's no such thing, 'twas never in the
   place,
Except the stool I sit upon—and that's an old gin-case.
It does us for a safe as well, but you must keep it shut,
Or the flies would make it canter round the old bark hut.

I've seen the rain come in this hut just like a perfect flood,
Especially through that great big hole where once the
   table stood.
There's not a blessed spot, me boys, where you could lay
   your nut,
But the rain is sure to find you in the old bark hut.

So beside the fire I make my bed, and there I lay me down,
And think myself as happy as the king that wears a crown.
But as you'd be dozing off to sleep a flea will wake you up,
Which makes you curse the vermin in the old bark hut.

So now, my friends, I've sung my song, and that as well
   as I could,
And I hope the ladies present won't think my language
   rude,
And all ye younger people, in the days when you grow up,
Remember Bob the Swagman, and the old bark hut.

From *Old Bush Songs*

THE LONG LONG
ARM OF THE LAW

IN THE SMALL HOURS OF SUNDAY MORNING,
2 September 1894, Senior Constable Michael Daly
was on patrol outside Dagworth woolshed. The
labour unrest was taken so seriously by the authorities in Brisbane that they had sent police to watch
outback stations—where shearing sheds were vul-
nerable to arson—and outback townships where
unionists gathered.

Michael Daly noticed nothing amiss till a
shot rang out and hit the hut where he normally
slept. He exchanged fire with the attackers and
managed to get to the hut. Then with two of the
defenders, he made it to the cover of a heap of
earth, where they kept on firing at attackers 40 or
50 yards away. Meanwhile Bob Macpherson who
was trying to get to the shed gave up in the face of
hostile fire.

The attackers' strategy of tying the defenders up in a gun battle succeeded completely by preventing them from saving the shed. Soon after the shooting began, one of the strikers had started the fire that destroyed most of the shed, and the lambs in their pens. This man is believed to have been Samuel Hoffmeister, born in Germany and generally known as Frenchy, who came from Springsure (on the other side of Barcaldine), a member of the striking shearer's union, and to those who knew him—'a bit mad'. In the bad light no one saw him at his dastardly work, but next day's events give reason to suspect him.

Their mission accomplished, the attackers disappeared in the night while steady rain obliterated their tracks. Next morning Michael Daly and Bob Macpherson rode for Kynuna township, 20 miles off. Two police were temporarily posted there to keep an eye on the many unionists camped nearby. They were among hundreds of police who extended in a thin blue line around the inland areas during the troubled times: a solid commitment in the sparsely populated backblocks.

In his 1902 poem 'The Old Australian Ways' Banjo would write wistfully of the attractions of country beyond the law, which Clancy had reached when he 'took the drovers track in years of long ago':

And if it be that you would ride
    The tracks he used to ride,
Then you must saddle up and go
    Beyond the Queensland side—
Beyond the reach of rule or law,
    To ride the long day through,
In Nature's homestead—filled with awe
Then you might see what Clancy saw
    And know what Clancy knew.

Vol. II, p. 142

The truth is that in colonial Australia it was no easy matter to out-reach rule or law. Government arrived straight after the first settlers; colonial government with its inspectors, policemen, forms to fill in and hands outstretched, in its most fundamental office, the raising of revenue.

To lament this intrusion is a time-honoured task of poets; and to complain about the reach of government is naturally ingrained in the human psyche. Thousands of years ago in China, when large parts were still awaiting settlement, Confucius travelled along an outback road and noticed a woman weeping at the roadside. Stepping down from his carriage he knelt with her beside the grave she was facing. After compassionately weeping a while, he asked what had happened. 'This is the grave of my husband. He was killed by a tiger,' she sobbed. A little longer, and he asked about the grave on the left. In a fresh torrent of tears she identified the grave of her father, 'also killed by a tiger'. What about the grave on the right? 'There lies my child, killed by a tiger.'

Confucius asked why her family chose to live where the tigers were so menacing. 'Out here, she said, 'the government doesn't bother us.'

Her descendents, on the admittedly dubious assumption that she had descendents, would have been safer from tigers, but no doubt they muttered about the passing of the good old days every time the government interfered in their lives.

Few governments in world history have established authority as quickly over new territory as the Queensland Government, which opened for business in 1859 and by the 1890s had over a million square kilometres under contribution and regular inspection. In the back country the government's most visible manifestation was the police force.

Australia—in contrast with other countries when they were newly settled, South America and the USA are obvious comparisons—is notable for the rapid spread of law and centralised order. Settlers came hot on the heels of explorers, and close behind them, came policemen and magistrates.

While people often complained about the ubiquitous presence of the law, it is clearly one of the factors that made Australia a safe and pleasant country to live in. The colonial authorities ensured that in their jurisdictions, might did not equate with right; the Wild West, where communities took the law into their own hands, was not part of Queensland—at least not for more than about 18 months. The gun-slinging violence that still infests the USA, and the failure of civil authority seen through much of South America are not Australian problems, and we should appreciate the large part the colonial police played in ensuring that they couldn't take root. Looking back, it's a pity in fact that the net of the law wasn't spread even earlier, to prevent some of the shocking initial clashes between whites and blacks on the frontiers of settlement.

Sometimes the jobs people do are influenced by the faith they profess. The people of country Queensland were not a devout bunch, but religious affiliation played a more decisive part in career paths then than now. There was nothing written down about it; if you were a Protestant you just knew that the Queensland Police Force was not the employer for you. Whether Catholicism was the strongest recommendation for service, or Irish ancestry, the Force was ethnically uniform and religiously consistent. In the bush, a significant exception was made for Aborigines. If you were an Aborigine, your legendary tracking skills could get you into a uniform—though never a promotion. And in the crises of 1891 and 1894, many and various temporary special constables were signed on in large numbers, without the usual regard to their faith and ancestry.

Perhaps the homogeneity of the Force promoted its esprit de corps and efficiency, which were pretty good considering its brief history. The police showed no hesitation in protecting the property of squatters, who were nearly all Protestants, albeit not the churchgoing kind.

So it was that Senior Constable Michael Daly rode into Kynuna that Sunday with Bob Macpherson, manager of Dagworth. Another squatter came in on the same day—Samuel McColl McCowan, manager of nearby Kynuna station. He brought news of a swagman who had killed himself at a nearby billabong.

Macpherson and Daly set out back towards Dagworth with the two Kynuna policemen, Senior Constables Dyer and Cafferty. A few miles downstream they turned off to the billabong where the suicide had occurred. The seven unionists still camped there beheld the unusual spectacle of a squatter riding down with not one but three policemen. They showed the police the body of Frenchy Hoffmeister, shot in the mouth and lying, with his gun, by the billabong.

All seven were arrested and held in custody in Kynuna for the coronial enquiry into Hoffmeister's death, conducted by magistrate Ernest Eglinton a few days later. At that hearing the union shearers gave evidence that Hoffmeister had been behaving oddly (even for him) that Sunday morning: pacing up and down, ostentatiously burning a letter, and moving away out of sight, just before they heard the shot that killed him.

Perhaps his conscience, weighed down with the enormity of the shed burning and shoot out, drove him to suicidal despair; the answer to that speculation died with him. One of his fellow campers rode to Kynuna station to let McCowan know what had happened. This was a self-sacrificing gesture of respect for their dead mate, because it drew onto the surviving seven the prime suspicion for the shooting and arson.

They had all been camped 4 miles out of Kynuna, at the end of a direct track to Dagworth woolshed. The bulk of the unionists were camped miles away, next to the township of Kynuna. The suspects claimed they had had to camp separately to have grass for their horses, but in fact there was plenty of grass at Kynuna.

Most of the men arrested at that billabong had prior convictions; but after the inquest they were set free, never to be prosecuted for the shooting or arson.

It wouldn't have been easy to get a conviction without evidence identifying the night raiding party at Dagworth woolshed. But the decision to let them off may also have been part of a plan to settle matters for good. Something like that happened after the Eureka Rebellion was put down in Victoria in 1854. No one arrested at the Eureka Stockade hung for treason, or served the gaol terms laid down for sedition. Most were acquitted of various charges and ultimately a general amnesty was granted to all the rebels; not long afterwards, one of the ringleaders actually became a member of parliament.

It's quite possible that similar clemency was part of the unwritten arrangements for putting an end to the violence and destruction in Queensland. In any case no sheds were burnt after that and no shots were fired at any disputant after the bullet that Frenchy Hoffmeister used to end his life.

MAKING A SONG

SHEARING AT DAGWORTH'S REBUILT SHED was all finished, at the low rate of pay, by mid-December, and soon afterwards, the Macpherson brothers were reunited with their father and their sisters Chris and Jean, who all arrived from Melbourne. It seems unlikely though that Christmas 1894 was a merry one at the homestead. The recent death of Alice Macpherson, their wife and mother, must have cast a sombre atmosphere over the new family home.

Probably everyone was glad when the poet from Sydney dropped in on their isolated lives. Now they had a genial, witty, cultivated guest to show around, who also happened to be a good bushman, with an eye for fast horses—an enthusiasm he shared with his hosts.

They may not have known a lot about him to start with. Sarah Riley would have introduced Bartie Paterson, rather than Banjo the *Bulletin* poet. It wouldn't have taken long to explain that they were one man, but it's also likely that his new friends didn't know much about his work. The *Bulletin* was one of two very good weekly papers with national circulation and a strong appeal in the bush. The Macphersons were more likely readers of the *Bulletin's* highbrow rival from Melbourne, the *Australasian,* which was very different: respectable, while the *Bulletin* was outrageous; open minded and politically conservative, while the *Bulletin* was progressive and prejudiced. The two papers paired up really well but they were probably read more often singly. The *Australasian* tended to be identified with landed wealth the way the *Bulletin* was with the working man.

As for Banjo Paterson, he didn't fit any of these moulds. Writer for the *Bulletin* and son of the squattocracy, once he was out of the city, he identified with everyone.

Banjo's visit was not the only excitement in the district, according to a talk he gave on radio in the 1930s. 'Golden Water' describes the success of the new artesian bores going in at that time: a factor he proposed as an influence on 'Waltzing Matilda'.

I do not know that I have properly conveyed the feeling of excitability which possessed everybody in the early days of the bore water: people seemed to be looking out on to limitless horizons and except (very occasionally) in a mining camp, I can remember nothing like it. The shearers staged a strike by way of expressing themselves, and Macpherson's woolshed at Dagworth was burnt down and a man was picked up dead. This engendered no malice and I have seen the Macphersons handing out champagne through a pub window to these very shearers. And here a personal reminiscence may be worth recording. While resting for lunch or while changing horses on our four-in-hand journeys, Miss Macpherson... used to play a little Scottish tune on a zither and I put words to the tune and called it 'Waltzing Matilda'. Not a very great literary achievement perhaps, but it has been sung in many parts of the world. It was the effect of the bore water.

Vol. II, p. 498

Banjo was very inquisitive—always on the lookout for fresh material and insights into bush life. He joined the Macphersons on their excursions to Winton, other stations and Kynuna. He learnt all about the recent labour dispute, and Frenchy's suicide. He would also have heard stories about a man who drowned, a few years earlier, in the bore hole of the Dagworth wool scour, and of a man on Manuka station who had drowned accidentally in a billabong. Researchers who have tried to confirm that story in official records conclude that it never happened. But if the story was going around, it would still have entered Banjo's mind with all the other facts and fables he was gathering from the district.

He met Jack Lawton, the horse breaker at Dagworth, who was to become a long-term friend. They met again in South Africa, when Lawton was attached to the Queensland forces in the Boer War, and Paterson was a correspondent. In Australia Lawton rode horses for Banjo including his steeplechase winner, Crusader.

They used to talk about 'Waltzing Matilda' in later years, and in Lawton's family there were reminiscences of the Dagworth days. His daughter Rita Brownridge wrote to the researcher and 'Waltzing Matilda' expert Richard Magoffin (1937–2006) on 8 March 1972, describing one of the family outings that included Lawton and Paterson:

> As they were driving along the road Bango
> Patterson saw a swagman coming along

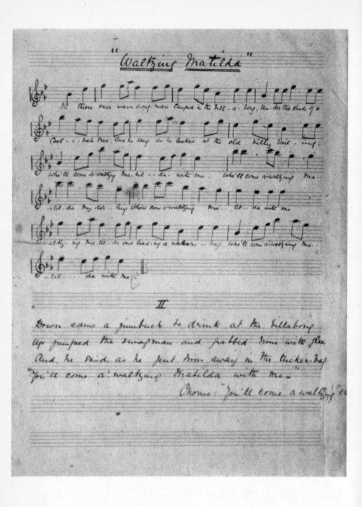

The 1895 version in Christina Macpherson's hand—a copy given to Mr and Mrs W. B. Bartlam at the Winton Race Carnival, May 1895, and now held by the National Library.

III

Down came the squatter a-riding his thoroughbred.
Down came policemen one, two, and three;
"Whose is the jumbuck you've got in the tucker-bag?
You'll come a-waltzing Matilda with we."

Chorus: You'll come a-waltzing &c

IV

But the swagman he ups and he jumped in the water-hole
Drowning himself by the Coolibah tree.
And his ghost may be heard as it sings by the billabong
Who'll come a-waltzing Matilda with me!

Chorus: "Who'll come a-waltzing &c

carrying his swag, or his bluey as they
sometimes called it and his black billy can,
he asked Bob McPherson to explain, why
they lived this kind of life.

Bob answered that the swagmen could always
get rations from the stations and described a practice that annoyed him: 'they would kill a sheep and
only take as much as they could carry away with
them, and leave the rest to rot in the sun, bringing
flies and disease'.

One evening at the homestead, the overseer, Jack
Carter, came in late for dinner, and Bob asked if
he'd seen anything of note that day. 'No,' he replied,
'only a waltzing matilda.' Banjo asked what he
meant and Carter explained that he'd noticed a
swagman and that waltzing matilda means travelling with a swag. Some have explained the novelty
of the term by suggesting it was understood in parts
of Victoria and Queensland, but hardly known in
New South Wales. Banjo would fix that.

Another new experience was the tune that
Chris Macpherson played. In her letter to Thomas
Wood she remembers the effect it had:

We went into Winton for a week or so and
one day I played (from ear) a tune which I
had heard played by a band at the Races in

Warrnambool…Mr Paterson asked what it
was. I could not tell him, and he then said he
thought he could write some lines to it. He
then and there wrote the first verse. We tried
it and thought it went well, so he then wrote
the other verses. I might add that in a short
time everyone in the district was singing it.

It seems she recalls working the song out in
Winton. Like many a song it must have taken
inventing and finishing at more than one time and
place. Banjo later told his friend Vince Kelly what
he thought when he heard Chris's tune:

It was such a catchy, whimsical, provocative
tune that I said to her 'Why don't you sing
the words to that?'
    She replied 'It hasn't got any words that I
know of, but it must have had at one time. I
believe it was an old Scottish hymn.'
    It was then that I decided it should have
words to keep it alive…I wrote words which
I thought expressed its whimsicality and
dreaminess.

The zither he heard Chris playing was a special
sort: an autoharp, which belonged to the book-
keeper at Dagworth. An autoharp has many strings,

and lies horizontally, like a xylophone. Its special feature is dampers, like a piano has, but worked by hand. A good operator can probably get a lot of control over notes and chords, but it isn't the first instrument you'd choose to recreate a piece of brass band music. In the process, the tune from Christina's memory underwent a transformation.

She was probably obliged to pluck a one-handed melody, slowing down and simplifying the rhythm. This happened to suit the whimsicality of the new piece as it was in 1895. Now we have a more rollicking tune, and we can only get the haunting feel it used to have by slowing down, and drawing out the syllables. Nothing in the way of ornament or accompaniment goes back to Dagworth, just a bare melody. At that stage nothing was written down except the words. When Chris later wrote out the score it proved scarcely playable on most instruments. To play her original 1895 melody and sing to it, you have to adjust the register and the rhythm.

Then the effect of the music and words is just as Banjo described: catchy, whimsical and dreamy. The resemblance to the currently popular tune and words is obvious, but the effect is quite different. The difference in rhythm is also apparent in the original words, which survive in a few handwritten copies and can now be considered, line by line.

Oh there once was a swagman camped in the billabongs

Depending which copy you look at, the text says 'billabong', or 'billabongs' in the plural. Richard Magoffin considers that the final 's' is mistaken and that Banjo meant to specify the billabong where Frenchy Hoffmeister shot himself. That has a tiny island in it with a coolibah tree on top, so that when the water level is right down, you can camp *in* it and still be under the tree's shade. That supports his claim that 'Waltzing Matilda' is about a specific swagman. However even with the water right down, the island and its surrounds mightn't make an attractive camp site, and with the water right down, diving into the puddle remaining would look like a slapstick routine. The alternative reading 'in the billabongs' makes sense if it means in amongst the billabongs—there being plenty of places along the Diamantina with paired or grouped billabongs. It doesn't rule out the billabong where Frenchy camped, which has another billabong alongside.

The Aboriginal word *billabong* is a compound. *Billa* means water in many dialects, and quite a few New South Wales place names end in billa or billy. *Bong* (also pronounced *bung*) is a widespread word for dead. Nowadays we mainly use it for machines and body parts, as in the complaint 'my knee's gone bung'. But a billabong is not permanently stagnant, as a writer to the *Bulletin* explained on 7 March 1896:

> 'Billabong' does not signify a pond of dead motionless water. It is the aboriginal equivalent of 'ana-branch'—a natural by-wash or secondary channel, running, as a rule only in flood-time. The Billabong Creek is a billabong of the Murray...A billabong may form the flood connection of two separate rivers; the Willandra Billabong is an example. But there is as much difference between a billabong and a lagoon as between a State-bank and a Mercantile; and the integrity of the aboriginal term should be preserved.

These words are signed Tom Collins, which is the nom de plume of the great Joseph Furphy, author of *Such is Life*. He knew billabongs in the Riverina; there are more in Queensland because in the wet, the shallow rivers spread into countless secondary courses. When these secondary flows subside, every waterhole in the subsidiary channels is left storing water.

Under the shade of a Coolibah tree;
And he sang as he looked at the old billy boiling,

According to some, this is a special billy, as to which, see the next chapter.

Who'll come a-waltzing Matilda with me.

A matilda is a swag. In 1893 Henry Lawson had commented on a similar term but less lyrical than waltzing matilda in 'Some Popular Australian Mistakes':

> A swag is not generally referred to as a
> 'bluey' or 'Matilda'—it is *called* a
> 'swag'…No bushman thinks of 'going on the
> wallaby' or 'walking Matilda' or 'padding
> the hoof'; he goes on the track—when forced
> to it.
>
> *Bulletin*, 18 November 1893

Lawson has a point, but some bushmen did speak of waltzing matilda, at least in more expressive moments. No doubt the grim humour of it appealed to men plodding for ages far from female company and ballroom glamour. It is thought to have been a Victorian term, naturally enough transplanted to Queensland, but not New South Wales, where Lawson and Paterson heard it imperfectly or missed it.

In Norse legend, Mathilda was a battle maid, buxom, beaming and brutal. In some countries, the ladies who follow armies around came to be known in a lampooning way as matildas. Usually though a soldier must march and camp without female company and with jocular glumness the name 'Matilda' was transferred to the limited resources on hand for supplying warmth and comfort—in some cases to the bag in which the soldier carried his bedding; in others, to his great coat.

For several centuries in Europe there has been a custom applied to tradesmen newly released from their indentures; they became journeymen, which means travelling around the country plying their trade and eking a living from customers and the generosity of local businesses—a bit like going on the wallaby for 18 months. If a journeyman was able to induce a girl to come along and keep him company, she was known as his Matilda, by analogy between military and civilian life. Analogy again led to his pack of bedding and possessions being called matilda. The custom apparently is still kept up in some trades. In Germany where it was all but snuffed out by World War II, there used to be hundreds or thousands of these journeymen on the track. This is called being *auf der walze*. Matilda is not a German name, but apparently it was borrowed for German journeymen, who sometimes went *auf der walze mathilde*.

It seems highly likely that German diggers brought the term to the Victorian goldfields in the 1850s and 1860s.

Who'll come a-waltzing Matilda, my darling
Who'll come a-waltzing Matilda with me
Waltzing Matilda and leading a water-bag
Who'll come a-waltzing Matilda with me.

The chorus introduces a waterbag, which was carried on a stick fed through its ears. This is sometimes called leading a waterbag, which sounds like the sort of term to take Banjo's fancy.

Up came the jumbuck to drink at the water-hole,

Jumbuck is probably also Victorian; an Aboriginal word for sheep—derived, say some, from the word for a small marsupial with minimal resemblance to a sheep, or, say others, from *dombok,* a white mist.

Up jumped the swagman and grabbed him in glee;

Some versions say 'with glee', which singers always prefer.

And he said as he put him away in the tucker-bag
'You'll come a-waltzing Matilda with me.'

The final line of verse two is an instruction to the jumbuck's remains. Some listeners imagine that the whole jumbuck goes into the bag but that would be impossible; by this stage the carcase has been butchered, and chosen cuts will be all that fit.

Up came the squatter, a-riding his thoroughbred;

Squatters like Bob Macpherson were enthusiasts for fast horses that they entered in country race meetings and used for personal transport the rest of the time.

Up came policemen—one, two and three

'Policemen' was changed to 'troopers' early on, for poetic advantage. A commentator has suggested that one specific trooper was meant—three being excessive to patrol a paddock—and that his service number had been '123'. Magoffin researched this and found that number 123 in the Queensland Police was Acting Sergeant Gallagher, who had a coastal posting in 1867. He cannot be our man, and clearly it was always meant to be three. Three police had gone with Bob to the billabong where Frenchy killed himself.

**'Whose is that jumbuck you've got in the tucker-bag?
You'll come a-waltzing Matilda with we.'**

It says 'we' because the poor swaggy was outnumbered by the people trying to arrest him. 'We' is only in the earliest versions, because singers didn't like it.

**Up sprang the swagman and jumped in the
water-hole,
Drowning himself by the Coolibah tree;
And his voice can be heard as it sings in the
billabongs
'Who'll come a-waltzing Matilda with me.'**

Some copies say 'ghost' instead of 'voice'.
The song travelled quickly to the outside world. Magoffin believes it was sung when the reconciliation of the squatters and the union was celebrated

in January 1895 at the Kynuna Hotel. Tradition has it that it was for this occasion that Bob Macpherson shouted French champagne, handing it in to the union shearers in the public bar.

If the new song wasn't sung then, and there's no way to know, its first public airing might have been in Winton. Helen Anderson (née Morrison) was a child at Ayrshire Downs—the overnight stop en route from Dagworth to Winton. She remembered Banjo coming into the nursery during such a stopover when he was on his way to town with the Macphersons. He read 'Waltzing Matilda' to the children. She believed he then went to stay with Fred Riley in Vindex Street and sang the words that evening to Marie Riley's piano accompaniment. She had heard that a few days later it was sung at the North Gregory Hotel by Herbert (later Sir Herbert) Ramsay, whose family owned nearby Oondooroo station. Herbert Ramsay was the best singer in the district. Like others from those parts he later went into politics.

Rita Brownridge, whose father went to Winton with Banjo, puts it the other way round: that they stayed at the North Gregory Hotel and went to the parlour, where Christina 'sat to the piano and picked out the tune' and it was sung there; that later Herbert Ramsay sang it at a party at the Riley's place.

It took off after that and travelled far and wide through inland Queensland, changing as it went. People picked it up by ear and reconstructed it with their own ideas about ornamentation and tempo. It may have got quicker as it did the rounds of pubs and country dances. Late in 1895 when Banjo was again in the area, and visiting Oondooroo with Christina and Bob, they dressed Herbert up as a swagman, got him to sing it, and took photos (which are lost).

In 1900 when the Governor, Lord Lamington, visited Winton, at the VIP dinner at the Post Office Hotel, he requested the song. Herbert obliged, and the whole company joined in the chorus.

At some point in these early days the line 'Drowning himself by the Coolibah tree' disappeared from the oral tradition, replaced by the defiant and ever popular 'You'll never catch me alive said he'.

In 1902 'Waltzing Matilda' was the theme song for town celebrations at Hughenden. The local paper printed the words and they were distributed on leaflets so the whole town could erupt in song.

While the song went from strength to strength, things weren't all onwards and upwards for the Macphersons. Jean married a squatter—McCowan from neighbouring Kynuna.

Bob didn't marry. He had an affair with a French musician, Josephine Pene. They had a son and as Bob had declined to marry her, she found a different way to let the world know of his parentage. She named the poor little bloke Dagworth Robert Rutherford Macpherson Pene.

In 1906 Bob gave up the battle with debt and drought and abandoned Dagworth to the mortgagees. For a while he got work managing a station near Cloncurry. He spent a lot of time in Cloncurry at the home of Josephine and his son, and something that drew them all together was music. They had many happy hours round the piano, and no doubt 'Waltzing Matilda' was prominent in their repertoire. Bob had a variety of work after that. He was living in a hut attached to his job as inspector of the rabbit-proof fence in 1930, when he suffered a heart attack at Kynuna Hotel and died.

Christina didn't marry either. She only stayed in Queensland for about a year. She went back to Melbourne and lived there in modest circumstances until her death in 1936.

After a few weeks Banjo left the district with its new song, and went home to Sydney. But he returned several times in the 1890s and kept his fond memories of Waltzing Matilda country for the rest of his life.

Banjo's engagement to Sarah Riley did not last, and she went to England. There has been plenty of speculation about things in Queensland that might have driven them apart, but nothing based on anything either of them said or wrote. No one has considered whether Banjo's novel *An Outback Marriage* sheds light on the question.

The novel, finished in 1899 or 1900, is largely based on personal experiences. It can be read as autobiographical fiction, with Banjo's characteristics apportioned among three very different characters. Part of the novel is set in outback Queensland.

Other action takes place in the high country of New South Wales. The unscrupulous young solicitor, Blake, has been unofficially engaged for years to Ellen, governess at Kuryong, a station up there. Visiting Kuryong, Blake finds himself enchanted by the singing voice of the squatter's daughter Mary Grant. He begins courting her immediately, and next morning breaks off with Ellen.

In a narrative drawn from life, Blake could have taken the place of Bartie, Ellen of Sarah and Mary of Christina, but that is all guesswork. We learn that the lawyer had never been in love with Ellen, although happy enough at the idea of marrying her.

This novel has a noticeable way of making you sympathise with the plight and aspirations of all the characters, even those with personal failings or criminal methods. In much the same way, Banjo may have felt for the people whose lives he complicated up in Queensland. Blake's hopes of winning Mary Grant come to naught in *An Outback Marriage,* which you could say mirrors Paterson's departure from Queensland with neither Sarah nor Christina as a romantic prospect.

There is nothing else to affirm the implication that any feeling between Banjo and Chris busted his ties with Sarah. In correspondence he is described as a model gentleman; also as attractive to women, and a heartless flirt. One letter writer says he 'jilted' Sarah; another, cryptically, suggests she had to drop him because of the attentions he paid to the sewing mistress at Dagworth.

Some of these matters may be relevant to knowledge of 'Waltzing Matilda'.

There is an alternative tune, suited to the Queensland words, known to some as the 'Buderim tune' and to others as the 'Queensland' or 'Cloncurry tune'. A fine tune it is and still sometimes played and recorded. It is not widely known that a New South Wales song, 'Our School Blaxland East', is set to the same music.

For a long time no one had any idea where this tune came from, but it is considered likely that it originated in Cloncurry on Josephine Pene's piano; perhaps she was being driven up the wall by Bob's relentless singing to Chris's melody, and decided to give him a completely different alternative.

Despite the falling out with Sarah, Banjo for a while kept in contact with the Riley and Macpherson families. In 1902 he wrote from Sydney asking Chris if she could send him a score of her Waltzing Matilda tune, and to say he had given it to a musical friend.

The friend would have been James Inglis, proprietor of the Billy Tea Co. Marie Cowan (1835–1919), wife of Inglis's manager, finished up with the job in 1903 of rewriting 'Waltzing Matilda' to promote Billy Tea. The words and music we have today, in which 'Waltzing Matilda' rose to national pre-eminence and global prominence, are not those of Banjo's first version, nor of Josephine Pene, nor Chris Macpherson. They are amendments of Marie Cowan's arrangement of music and words, done in Sydney in 1903.

WHAT DOES IT MEAN?

ONE OF THE FIRST THINGS YOU NOTICE about 'Waltzing Matilda', if you pay attention to the words, is the absurdity of the little tale it tells. 'Jolly' is a nonsense word introduced to the lyrics by Marie Cowan—probably to make the swagman seem happier about his tea and to stand in for a less polite description of the jumbuck. But go back to Banjo's 1895 original and you will see that at face value 'Waltzing Matilda' was absurd, *ab initio*.

A station is half a million acres. The squatter employs a staff of boundary riders, station hands, jackaroos and overseers, and runs 100,000 sheep; he does not attend in person at the demise of just one of them. The police are responsible to keep the peace throughout an extensive country with plenty of real work to do. They don't have three troopers on the spot in an outback paddock to apprehend a lone swagman for stealing a single sheep. The swagman has seen a lot of ups and downs while travelling through the land. He wouldn't let a little bother with the law ring the cut out bell on his career. Even if he had previous convictions, a brief term in prison was the worst he had to fear for his minor offence. The billabong is a shallow body of still water. It doesn't drown a man unless he is unconscious, or someone is holding him under. It would be a muddy but straightforward procedure for a squatter and three troopers to drag the fugitive out.

So perceptive readers naturally conclude that there is something else going on in the song—something more than the implausible narrative on the surface.

In this they are encouraged by the realistic tone of Banjo's other tales. Like any decent poet he could improve on the facts—to improve on the story, or make the funny side more obvious. But even at their most far fetched his poems are believable, with no more adjustment than a reader normally makes to accommodate a doubt.

Clearly then this song deliberately was different, and readers frequently find a fable in it, and sometimes seek a message or a moral. The voice that is heard when you pass by the billabong might be a protest at unfairness in the world.

Perhaps the squatter stands for the affluent and greedy, begrudging the poor a little of their wealth. The troopers then must be the state's repressive arm, working in collusion with upper-class interests. And the swagman speaks for all of those who want a better deal from life but have no option left except despair.

But when looking for politics in 'Waltzing Matilda' it's easier to see a protest than a message. If the swagman is a hero, he's hardly one to emulate—not for a listener with a future at least. He isn't even easy to admire. Someone who'd commend him for stealing a jumbuck still might not see in his self-imposed drowning the sign of courage or wisdom, or other noble qualities.

It doesn't sound like Paterson to invite reprisals against property owners or authority, but if he really meant singers to avenge the swagman's death, he could at least have given the squatter and troopers a more culpable participation in the poor man's undoing.

Following this line of enquiry increasingly looks hopeless without some key to unlock the mystery of the song, otherwise we seem to drift around with nothing exact to go on.

There is someone who offers a key: who goes beyond the baffling words into the background against which the song might have been composed. Richard Magoffin argues strongly for a quite specific political interpretation. His grandfather, also Richard Magoffin, had Quambetook station—which for a while shared a boundary with Dagworth—and was a friend of Bob Macpherson. Still living there in the 1960s, the younger Magoffin researched the origins of 'Waltzing Matilda' very thoroughly, speaking and writing to many old people with memories of parts of the story. Before it was too late he was able to reconstruct the genesis of 'Waltzing Matilda'.

His book *Fair Dinkum Matilda* (1973) described the political allegory locked in the lines of 'Waltzing Matilda', a theme he has developed and promoted ever since.

Magoffin went back to a poem published in *The Worker* during the first round of labour unrest in 1891. That journal was the organ of the striking workers, edited by William Lane (1861–1917). Lane was a dreamer and a vocal advocate of worker's rights. Later he would lead a group of visionaries to establish a utopian commune in Paraguay, where he aimed to implement the socialist paradise that Australia had denied him.

In May 1891 he published 'Freedom on the Wallaby' by Henry Lawson, which refers to a billy in the final stanza:

But Freedom's on the wallaby
She'll knock the tyrants silly
She's going to light another fire
And boil another billy.
We'll make the tyrants feel the sting
Of those that they would throttle;
They needn't say the fault is ours
If blood should stain the wattle.

According to Magoffin it is this other billy that Banjo sings about as 'the old billy boiling', in the first verse of 'Waltzing Matilda'. So Magoffin interprets 'Waltzing Matilda' as a response to 'Freedom on the Wallaby'. The 1891 trouble was bubbling up again in 1894. The old billy was boiling, and that must be why it was 'the', and not 'his', billy in 'Waltzing Matilda'.

For Lawson, the repression of the workers and the denial of labour rights broke the promise of a fair deal for all Australians, chaining the workers to the same sort of privileged interests that held the lower classes in thrall overseas.

While the labour movement was losing one campaign, Lawson was adamant that the issue must not go away—the billy would boil again, and the oppressors might regret it.

In 1891 Henry Lawson was already a writer with a following whose work in the *Bulletin* was eagerly read. He didn't have Paterson's poetic gifts, but he had a clearer eye for the bleak side of life, and a fine talent for storytelling that made him the best short-story writer of his time, in Australia at least.

Many people were upset or deeply offended that a prominent writer should suggest that bloodshed might be justified by Australia's problems: some supporters of the labour cause thought Lawson went too far. In Queensland he was threatened with prosecution for sedition.

Because of the political tone in his work, his poverty and his liking to speak for the underprivileged, critics and historians generally class Lawson as the socialist, the left winger, in the literary dialogue. Banjo, the child of the squattocracy, with his positive outlook, is pigeonholed by some as a political conservative, sympathetic to employers and capital.

That account of Banjo's politics is at odds with his writing, and his sympathies range very obviously across the social spectrum from the horse thief to the prince. Villains are few in Paterson's writing; his hostility is reserved for British imperialism, for foreign interference and occasionally for the banks.

Although he was much less divisive than Lawson, it's doubtful there was much between them politically, and Magoffin goes so far as to cast Banjo as the more radical socialist. That seems a bold conclusion, but even without it, there's nothing politically inconsistent in Banjo carrying on Lawson's crudely inflammatory discourse in the more cautious form of an allegory. In his 1886 poem 'The Bushfire', Paterson had openly resorted to allegory to attack the English Government's response to Irish agitation for home rule. The British Empire became 'the Empire Run', an Australian sheep station, managed by Billy Gladstone.

The significance of the boiling 'billy' is described above. Now following Magoffin's guidance, we can summarise the other meanings in his allegorical 'Waltzing Matilda'.

The 'swagman', at his most corporeal, is Frenchy Hoffmeister, who actually committed suicide by a billabong that Banjo was shown when he visited a few months later. In a more general way, the swagman represents 'the free citizen, the itinerant with no vote, no award, no arbitration, standing for the union'.

The 'jumbuck' stands for the property of the British banks and squatters—or we might say, the contested wealth of the country, which one group did not want to share. Magoffin's interpretation is strengthened by 'The Bushfire'. The jumbucks there plainly stand for the wealth of English interests in Ireland, Scotland and Wales:

There's Welshman's Gully, Scotchman's Hill,
And Paddymelon Flat:
And all these places are renowned
For making jumbucks fat.

Vol. I, p. 42

The 'billabong' and the 'coolibah' are Australia.

The 'squatter', mounted, and the 'troopers three' are the haughty vested interests and the excessive use of authority to protect their wealth and dominance.

'His ghost' in early versions of the song was 'his voice'. Magoffin writes:

> It was that *voice* of the working people of
> Australia calling for a fair society. That is
> really what was *drowned* by that excess of
> authority: hundreds of police, soldiers, guns,
> backed by savage laws, which sent men to
> jail for long terms. They were silenced but
> that *voice* would eventually be heard.
>
> *The Provenance of Waltzing Matilda*, p. 5

Magoffin does more than just read the song as political allegory. He places Banjo Paterson in the thick of the events themselves. He asks, what was Banjo doing in the weeks he spent at Dagworth? Why did he repeatedly come back to the district?

Why did he say he was visiting Queensland 'on business'?

Even back in those days, when lawyers were less inclined to generate mountains of work, it wasn't easy or usual to leave your practice for weeks or months for holidays in Queensland. So Magoffin argues that Banjo was working there, to reconcile the squatters and unionists; and that he brought about a settlement. Late in 1894, before Banjo's arrival, the squatters had solved their main problem by finding enough shearers to work at the low rates they wanted to pay. But in 1895 while he was there the sheep needed crutching, and with so many sheep, even that was a big job requiring many shearers, at a time when not so many were still in the district. Banjo, respected by all, must have brought the parties to agreement, and also written his song against the backdrop of the labour negotiations.

The suggestion is plausible enough, but as Magoffin admitted, it is speculative, based on a fact here and a fact there. It is doubtful we'll ever know. But we don't need to, 'Waltzing Matilda' can be read as an allegory even if Banjo was just a bystander. 'The Bushfire' makes it easy to believe that with 'Waltzing Matilda' he had similar sport with bush symbolism in the context of the 1894 labour crisis.

One of the reasons people object to the political reading (and they do) is that 'Waltzing Matilda' is supposed to belong to everyone and to suit every occasion. They fear that attaching it to a historical event and making it the song of a particular political movement spoils its universality. 'It will remain our national folk song only for as long as no section of our community attempts to appropriate *Waltzing Matilda* as its own, as long as nobody attempts to capture and shape its history according to their own sectional standpoints,' write Magoffin's critics, Peter and Sheila Forrest. Objecting to Magoffin's focus on Frenchy Hoffmeister, the Forrests add: 'We do not want to know the identity of the man who lies in the tomb of the unknown soldier. Nor, for the same reasons, should we want to know the identity of the swagman'.

But accepting the Forrests' point about attempts to appropriate the song and about the advantage of the swagman's anonymity, there are two good reasons not to join them in discounting the political reading and historical specificity.

For one thing, the song doesn't take sides. People tend to read it as endorsement of the swagman's conduct or attitude; but if you wished you could find it a warning against law breaking and disrespect for others' property. Whether you hear it at face value or as a profound allegory, it tells a tale without declaring a judgement.

Secondly, the fact is that many, perhaps most, of the songs that live through the ages are born in specific circumstances, which they soon outgrow. Many are crystallised around a message that means little to later generations of singers.

A simple example is dozens of nursery rhymes we have inherited from past centuries: 'Three Blind Mice', 'Little Jack Horner', 'Humpty Dumpty' and 'Little Bo-Peep' all started out as political verses based on particular individuals. When a researcher nowadays pins down their origins and political orientation, it has no bearing on their continued value as children's entertainment, as resources for labelling current people and things, and as timeless truths, modern clichés and so on. 'Waltzing Matilda' is more complex, subtle and ingenious than a nursery rhyme. It can be interpreted, classified, claimed, honoured, denounced and explained without exhaustion, and without even diminishing its general appeal.

Banjo Paterson is an artist and frequently the works of artists are so created that they can be understood in different, even contradictory, ways. 'Waltzing Matilda' is like a magic mirror that will show you what you want when you look into it.

In the mind of an artist, perceptions and experiences mingle and grow into something new; the artist 'is not always aware of the whole experience involved nor the whole range of potential meaning. 'Waltzing Matilda' is like a dream. The episodes, people and pictures in the poet's mind are real, but they knit together in a new pattern, guided by Banjo's thoughts and feelings of the time.

Deliberately the artist leaves the work to react in the minds and senses of each member of the audience, to produce something individual and new. Whenever a work of literature is cryptic, mysterious or superficially baffling, it's highly likely to fall into that class.

In some cultures there are traditional writings that mean a lot more to people than the sentences express at face value. China has its *Tao Te Ching* by Lao Dzu. In Turkey, Iran, Syria and most other countries of western Asia there are many books and stories of a character named Hoja Nasrudin. Like the jolly swagman's, his actions seem contrary to good sense, although he tends to be comically dopey rather than suicidal. As with 'Waltzing Matilda' each reader has to look into the story to get the personal insight that it offers.

Clearly anyone trying to tell you that an interpretation of 'Waltzing Matilda' is not right has to

THE BUSHFIRE
An allegory

'Twas on the famous Empire run,
    Whose sun does never set,
Whose grass and water, so they say,
    Have never failed them yet—
They carry many million sheep,
    Through seasons dry and wet.

They call the homestead Albion House,
    And then, along with that,
There's Welshman's Gully, Scotchman's Hill,
    And Paddymelon Flat:
And all these places are renowned
    For making jumbucks fat.

And the out-paddocks—holy frost!
    There wouldn't be no sense
For me to try and tell you half—
    They really are immense;
A man might ride for days and weeks
    And never strike a fence.

But still for years they never had
    Been known a sheep to lose;
Old Billy Gladstone managed it,
    And you can bet your shoes
He'd scores of supers under him,
    And droves of jackaroos.

Old Billy had an eagle eye,
    And kept his wits about—

If any chaps got trespassing
    He quickly cleared 'em out;
And coves that used to 'work a cross',
    They hated him, no doubt.

But still he managed it in style,
    Until the times got dry,
And Billy gave the supers word
    To see and mind their eye—
'if any paddocks gets a-fire
    I'll know the reason why.'

Now on this point old Bill was sure,
    Because, for many a year,
Whenever times got dry at all,
    As sure as you are here,
The Paddymelon Flat got burnt,
    Which Bill thought rather queer.

He sent his smartest supers there
    To try and keep things right.
No use! The grass was always dry—
    They'd go to sleep at night,
And when they woke they'd go and find
    The whole concern alight.

One morning it was very hot—
    The sun rose in a haze;
Old Bill was cutting down some trees
    (One of his little ways);
A black boy came hot-foot to say
    The Flat was in a blaze.

Old Bill he swears a fearful oath
 And lets the tommy fall—
Says he: 'I'll take this business up,
 And fix it once for all;
If this goes on, the cursed run
 Will send us to the wall.'

So he withdrew his trespass suits—
 He'd one with Dutchy's boss—
In prosecutions criminal
 He entered *nolle pros.*,
But these were neither here nor there—
 They always meant a loss.

And off to Paddymelon Flat
 He started double-quick
Drayloads of men with lots of grog
 Lest heat should make them sick,
And all the strangers came around
 To see him do the trick.

And there the fire was flaming bright,
 For miles and miles it spread,
And many a sheep and horse and cow
 Were numbered with the dead—
The super came to meet Old Bill,
 And this is what he said:

'No use, to try to beat it out,
 'Twill dry you up like toast,
I've done as much as man can do,
 Although I never boast;

I think you'd better chuck it up,
    And let the jumbucks roast.'

Then Bill said just two words: 'You're sacked,'
    And pitches off his coat,
And wrenches down a blue-gum bough
    And clears his manly throat,
And into it like threshing wheat
    Right sturdily he smote

And beat the blazing grass until
    His shirt was dripping wet;
And all the people watched him there
    To see what luck he'd get,
'Gosh! Don't he make the cinders fly,'
    And, 'Golly, don't he sweat!'

But though they worked like Trojans all,
    The fire still went ahead
So far as you could see around;
    The very skies were red,
Sometimes the flames would start afresh,
    Just where they thought it dead.

His men, too, quarrelled 'mongst themselves,
    and some coves gave it best,
And some said, 'Light a fire in front,
    And burn from east to west'—
But Bill he still kept sloggin' in,
    And never took no rest.

Then, through the crowd a cornstalk kid
    Came ridin' to the spot;

Says he to Bill, "Now take a spell,
    You're lookin' very 'ot,
And if you'll only listen why,
    I'll tell you what is what.

'These coves as set your grass on fire,
    There ain't no mortal doubt,
I've seen 'em riding here and there,
    And pokin' round about;
It ain't no use your working here,
    Until you finds them out.

'See yonder where you beat the fire—
    It's blazin' up again,
And fires are starting right and left
    On Tipperary plain,
Beating them out is useless quite,
    Unless Heaven sends the rain.'

Then Bill, he turns upon the boy,
    'Oh, hold your tongue you pup!'
But a cinder blew across the creek
    While Bill stopped for a sup,
And fired the Albion paddocks, too—
    It was a bitter cup;
Old Bill's great heart was broke at last,
    He had to chuck it up.

Moral

The run is England's Empire great,
    The fire is the distress

That burns the stock they represent—
    Prosperity you'll guess.
And the blue-gum bough is the Home Rule Bill
    That's making such a mess.

And Ireland green of course I mean
    By Paddymelon Flat;
All men can see the fire of course,
    Spreads on at such a bat,
But who are setting it alight
    I cannot tell you that.

But this I think all men will see,
    And hold it very true—
'Don't quarrel with effects until
    The *cause* is brought to view.'
What is the cause? That cornstalk boy—
    He seemed to think he knew.

           Banjo Paterson, 12 June 1886, vol. I, p. 42

be taken with a grain of salt. Someone whose job requires him to deal with this issue is Geoff Willats-Bryan, manager of the Waltzing Matilda Centre in Winton. Naturally people look to the Centre as an authority on the song. But he declines the opportunity to cloak anyone's specific way of hearing it with the mantle of orthodoxy. 'The Centre is the guardian of "Waltzing Matilda", not the owner,' he says. 'All Australians own it and it means something to each of them in an individual way. But it can also take on a single purpose. When you hear 50,000 people singing it at a Bledisloe Cup match, every one of them knows the words and sings it with passion. At times like that it represents the Australian spirit. The Australian spirit is as relevant today as it was when the song was first sung, and the song is one of the things that keep it alive.'

For Willats-Bryan, the very fact that no one can claim it for an exclusive viewpoint, class or interest opens the door to a meaning that everybody is happy to accept. 'Some power in "Waltzing Matilda" fosters a pride in us—not simple patriotism, but the feeling that we all belong to a family. It can do that partly because it isn't threatening. Even though the song tells a confronting story, there is no hostility in it to anyone. If anything, its effect is a calming one.'

Certainly this is a remarkable virtue of the song: out of a strange, remote episode and a despairing action long ago, it sends something positive and intimate direct to the minds and feelings of millions of people here and now.

This positive quality offers a balance for some people when they think about what it is to be Australian. The negative view is constantly being reinforced by commentators who describe their country like an inverted world such as Alice came to through the looking glass. Such commentators actually speak of Australia as 'down under' or 'the antipodes'. Antipodes is the Greek word for 'opposite one's feet'; even some people who live in Australia have their minds and feet in the Northern Hemisphere, and talk as if we were upside down. They describe Australia as an empty country, populated only on a narrow coastal perimeter. Australians they describe as a nation of migrants, as though our real home is somewhere else.

Sounding through the chorus that delivers this jaundiced message, the call from the billabong is a reminder that Australian life has been going on for generations; that Australia is our home, the inland as much as the coast; and that even if there is a cosmic top and bottom, we are not the ones standing upside down.

CENTURIES IN
THE MAKING?

IN 1977 THE COMMONWEALTH GOVERN-
ment declared that Australia would finally have a
national anthem of its own. No longer making do
with 'God Save the Queen', the electorate would
choose one at a vote the following year.

There was quite a debate in the lead up to this
plebiscite: 'it has to be a tune from Australia', some
said; and they added that because its music comes
from somewhere else, that meant that 'Waltzing
Matilda' wouldn't do.

The idea that the tune isn't an Australian one is
traceable back to 1895. Chris Macpherson told
Banjo then that the tune she remembered was an
'old Scottish hymn'. In time the Scottish prototype
was plausibly identified—as 'Thou Bonnie Wood of
Craigielee' by Robert Tannahill. This was not a
hymn but a song that he composed in or about

1805. Tannahill (born in 1774) drowned himself in a lagoon in 1810. The music to his song was by his countryman James Barr (1781 to 1860). Few Australians knew the tune—and how it was identified as Chris Macpherson's prototype is a mystery that isn't easily solved. If she could not recall the name of music she remembered from races in Victoria, how did her contemporaries, away in outback Queensland, find out what it was? Yet Helen Anderson (née Morrison), who lived then on Ayrshire Downs station next to Dagworth, remembered that the tune 'was definitely known as "Craigalee" from the early days. Both Mother and Mrs Riley knew the tune'. Mrs Riley was Sarah's sister-in-law in Winton.

To this day, belief in a Scottish original remains firmly entrenched. The National Library, including the Macpherson score in its 'National Treasures' display, declares that it is 'universally agreed to be her adaptation of the Scottish folk song "Thou Bonnie Wood of Craigielea"'.

But this leaves us still with a bit of sorting out to do: that it isn't a folk song but the work of Barr and Tannahill. And 'universally agreed' is a big claim to make. You might decide whether you share in this universal agreement when you try the Scottish song—the first verse and the chorus go like this:

THOU BONNIE WOOD OF CRAIGIELEE

The broom, the briar, the birken bush,
Bloom bonnie o'er the flowery lea
And a' the sweets that ane can wish
Frae nature's hand are strewed on thee.

Thou bonnie wood o' Craigielee
Thou bonnie wood o' Craigielee
Near thee I've spent life's early day
And won my Mary's heart in thee.

Four more verses continue the metre, and the same sort of saccharine wording goes on to the end. If you want to try singing those words to a tune of 'Waltzing Matilda' it might be best to ensure for a start that nobody else can hear. It is not easy to accept James Barr as 'Waltzing Matilda's' composer, but differences in what one hears can mask a strong relationship between music of very different styles. Tracking down the origins of a tune can be hard because of the natural tendency to parcel music up. The music of one country, style or period sounds incompatible with that of the others.

But careful analysis can match a multitude of melodies and rhythms belonging to musical traditions remote from one another. Tunes and snatches more readily cross barriers in time and place, and the boundaries of taste, than lyrics cross a language barrier.

Wherever a resemblance is found we can ask whether far removed pieces of music have origins in common. Quite often it is just coincidence. And frequently a pattern will act on the human mind so that one thing sounds right in two or more entirely different contexts.

You may get to hear one of Liszt's Hungarian Rhapsodies played with a cadenza near the end sounding exactly like 'Waltzing Matilda'—and without a lapse in the classical style of Liszt.

Franz Liszt was born in 1811 in the eastern part of the Austrian Empire. From the age of nine till his death in 1886, he travelled round Europe pursuing his music career. More than a composer, he was a scholar of music, who set out to gather traditional tunes, especially in Hungary, land of his birth, subject at the time to the monarchy of Austria.

He reproduced melodies he'd gathered from the Gypsies, in 'Hungarian Rhapsodies' and several other works. A leading exponent now of Liszt's piano music is Geoffrey Tozer. That explains the presence, on occasion, of 'Waltzing Matilda' in the Hungarian Rhapsodies. Liszt only created the opportunity by putting a cadenza where an Australian virtuoso introduces a passage of his own.

'Waltzing Matilda' sounds strikingly at home amongst the Eastern European melodies.

Owing to some spectacular miscalculations, at the court of Vienna and on the battlefields of World War I, Austria today is a tiny republic. In land area and general significance it stands somewhere in between Victoria and Dagworth, two homes of the Macphersons. Yet it was for several centuries—and throughout the life of Liszt—one of Europe's leading powers, with extensive eastern provinces. Hungary belonged to it and several little countries that are Hungary's independent neighbours now.

The chapter 'Making a Song' discussed the German origins of the expression 'waltzing matilda', firmly established by Melbourne scholar Harry Pearce. Pearce went further than that: he claimed there was an antique waltzing matilda song in Germany, with a tune quite like its Australian counterpart. It must, he said, have reached Australia in colonial times, and become the old bush song that Banjo Paterson modified for his own 'Waltzing Matilda', in 1895.

No trace has been found of such a song, nor of a German 'Waltzing Matilda' nor transmissions from Germany in colonial times. The German original comes from Pearce's imagination, like a rabbit from a hat. But in his search for matching melodies Pearce uncovered several from other places including nations further east. A Czech lament, with modern wording, to a tune of indeterminate age, shows a strong similarity. So does 'Multi Ani Traiasca', as sung in the south-east of Romania—an old song used to welcome guests, though it's only briefly that the similarity subsists.

Pearce also quotes this letter from historian Martin Ellis:

One of the most curious experiences I have had with 'Matilda' was to hear a fairly approximate version of it played on a pan pipe, as nearly as it could be produced on such an eerie instrument, by a shepherd boy on the edges of the Taurus Mountains in Central Asia Minor. I jumped to the conclusion that it must have been introduced to Turkey during World War I. But I was assured in Airange Darbend that it was 'very old'. The shepherd boy was the son of a local blacksmith, a descendant of one of the old Bohemian smiths who set up along the route of the crusaders…And the smith himself vouched for the fact that the tune had been in Anatolia 'before the Turks came'.

On the Origins of Waltzing Matilda, p. 67

In modern Turkey, there are indeed descendants of Bohemian migrants, distant cousins of modern Czechs. Ellis's local witnesses lend weight to the idea that the tune was there before the Anzacs brought it to Turkey in 1915.

As for the notion that it's been played in Anatolia since medieval times, we're impressed that a modern-day blacksmith can vouch for it. We leave it to the most trusting historians to be convinced.

Before World War I, frontiers used to shift repeatedly, between the rival empires of the Austrians and the Turks.

The postage-stamp nations that lived in eastern parts of Austria—Slovaks, Slovenes, Romanians and Czechs—have local folk traditions, expressed richly in the music that so enchanted Liszt. Under the Emperor's lenient yoke, they shared provinces in harmony—while melody-loving Gypsies carried tunes across their borders. At war the marching nations camped by each other's side, under the flag of the Viennese regime, and they sang and shared tunes while they campaigned for the Emperor, as later on 'Waltzing Matilda' was sung.

Insurrections in the Empire, and European politics, called these multi-national armies to the Austrian cause. In 1703 a mutinous force—mostly Hungarian, but financed in part by Turkey and by France—was marching on Vienna, perhaps to the strains of one of the melodies preserved by Liszt in his 'Rhapsodies'. While they were being beaten off, other Hungarians, with comrades in arms from neighbouring lands, were stationed in Italy, Germany, Spain and some in the Low Countries, between Holland and France.

In the War of the Spanish Succession they fought for Emperor Leopold against Louis XIV, the self-styled 'Sun King' of France. Louis at the time was Europe's leading trouble maker, and had seated his grandson on the vacant throne of Spain.

The prospect of the monarchies of France and of Spain (with all their vast possessions in Europe and abroad) being united under Louis's hand was too much altogether for Austria to bear. Louis furthermore was flouting solemn promises, which bound him not to claim the Spanish throne for his heirs.

In 1701 Austria had marched against France. The following year, Britain and the Netherlands joined in the Austrian cause, led by Churchill, Earl of Marlborough. Men from Transylvania, from the Danube Valley and from Balkan villages near the Turkish frontier fought against France alongside recruits from Holland and England. Here in what is now Belgium and the Netherlands, the allies wisely trusted Marlborough to conduct their combined campaign. Britain never produced a more successful general. He marched east in 1705, to save the Austrian Empire from imminent disaster, by annihilating the forces of France at the famous Battle of Blenheim.

Some generals think first of the welfare of their soldiers; to them the life of every man is dear. Marlborough was not a general like that. His men were a resource he could use without regret, as long as he knew that the losses of his enemies would be harder for them to sustain than his had been for England.

It needed a lot of encouragement, a constant recruiting campaign, to coax more men from home and keep up the supply of cannon fodder to a leader such as him. It has been suggested that the soldiers' catchy marching songs were adapted to advertise the dubious glamour of service overseas.

This may seem, patient reader, to have led you on a detour, far from the shade of the coolibah tree. But a song about those times may help us to make clear enough what the relevance to 'Waltzing Matilda' could be.

The song on page 116 is akin to those European melodies. It's easy to envisage that if English soldiers were singing it so many centuries ago, that they took their rhythm, and their tune, from something being played and sung by their allies in the war—for example from those 'Austrians' who hailed from homelands further east.

Waltzing Matilda

*Christina Macpherson's tune arranged by R. Magoffin and
E. Berryman for The Towers Players. Copyright 1982.*

Craigielee

*Part of Godfrey Parker's 'Craigielee', published for
Thomas Bulch in Melbourne in 1883.*

The Bold Fusilier

*Part of 'The Bold Fusilier' as recalled by Kathleen
Cooper for Harry Pearce, c. 1962*

But the eastern European similarity is not the similarity that will impress you the most:

THE BOLD FUSILIER

A gay fusilier was marching down through Rochester,
Bound for the wars in the Low Country
And he cried as he tramped through the drear streets of
    Rochester,
'Who'll be a sojer for Marlb'ro with me?
'Who'll be a sojer, who'll be a sojer,
Who'll be a sojer for Marlb'ro with me?'
And he cried as he tramped through the drear streets of
    Rochester,
'Who'll be a sojer for Marlb'ro with me?'

The wars in the Low Country came a century earlier than 'Thou Bonnie Wood of Craigielee', yet 'The Bold Fusilier' seems much closer to home than the Tannahill work. So close is it to 'Waltzing Matilda' that a direct creative link is indisputable.

In Kent, south-east of London, Rochester was convenient, as a port of embarkation for soldiers from the south, en route across the English Channel to continental wars. The song mentions the drear streets, but Rochester's only dreary in the general way of English towns: there is nothing exceptional, and it may be that the dreariness is there to make the point that the fusilier was headed for something much more colourful.

Shared origins in Europe are the plainest explanation for the resemblances of 'The Bold Fusilier' to the Eastern European melodies gathered by Pearce—and the tune heard in Turkey by Ellis.

'The Bold Fusilier' is virtually unknown now, only ever mentioned when 'Waltzing Matilda' is discussed. But it does seem that once it must have been more popular, as writers have claimed at various points. John Gilmaur in a letter to *People* magazine on 25 September 1968 wrote that 'The Bold Fusilier' had become the recruiting song 'Marching with Marlborough', that it was still on sale in Sydney in the early 1900s and that he once had a copy of his own.

In 1944, in *The Story of Waltzing Matilda*, Sydney May relayed the story of a man, at home with his mother, who whistled 'Waltzing Matilda'—a song the whistler's mother had never heard. She said she was surprised to discover that her son knew the music of 'The Bold Fusilier'. In his second edition, May identifies the whistler as a member of the *Bulletin* staff, whose mother came from Rochester, and knew the words from there. In his book *On the Origins of Waltzing Matilda*, Harry Pearce quotes a letter he received in 1962. Kathleen Cooper who sent it explains how her grandfather learnt 'The Bold Fusilier' in England from his grandfather.

But Richard Magoffin—who knows more about Chris Macpherson than did Gilmaur, Pearce or

May—is absolutely positive that the tune in her head was not 'The Bold Fusilier' but her own recollection of the march 'Craigielee'.

With such an obvious match to explain away, how can he be so sure? Fortunately the programme for the carnival at Warrnambool in April 1894 survived in the files of the *Warrnambool Standard,* the paper that still serves its picturesque and prosperous city today. The programme lists all the musical numbers that the Garrison Artillery Band would play at the races each day. There is a name we recognise on the programme for Tuesday 24 April:

WARRNAMBOOL AMATEUR TURF CLUB
25th APRIL, 1894

HIS EXCELLENCY
THE GOVERNOR LORD HOPETOUN PRESENT

MUSIC BY THE TOWN BAND ON TUESDAY 24th
AND THURSDAY 26th APRIL, 1894.

MARCH	"CRAIGIELEA"
SCHOTTISCHE	"THE ARGYLE"
MARCH	"JEANNIE GRAY"
WALTZ	"AFTER THE BALL"
FANTASIA	OP. "BOHEMIAN GIRL"
QUADRILLES	"OLD TIMES"
GRAND MARCH	"BRAVE BARNABY"
SERENADE	"TWILIGHT WHISPERINGS"
MARCH	"THE JACOBITE"
GALOP	"O'ER THE DOWNS"

There's 'Craigielee', first on the list of pieces that the audience, Chris Macpherson among them, was going to hear played.

However firmly common sense says 'Fusilier', historical research keeps saying 'Craigielee' to anyone trying to discover which tune was the basis for 'Waltzing Matilda'. The gap to bridge looks just as great as when our rambling enquiry began.

The key to the puzzle is the changes people make to music as it spreads and evolves. 'Craigielee' is not the same as 'Thou Bonnie Wood of Craigielee'; and our words and tune today for 'Waltzing Matilda' are not quite Banjo's words from 1895, nor the tune that Chris Macpherson then composed.

The words now are usually closer to the 1903 version, quoted on pages 210–11. And today's favourite tune is derived from the 1903 tune, printed on page 126. Compare 'The Bold Fusilier' with the 1895 song and the 1903 song and you'll see that at first 'Waltzing Matilda' was not nearly as close as it later became to 'The Bold Fusilier'.

But it was miles away already from 'Thou Bonnie Wood' of Tannahill and Barr. Luckily there are copies still of the score the band in Warrnambool must have used when it was playing 'Craigielee'. This music, which is printed on page 115, was published by Lyon's Music Store in Melbourne in 1893. It represents Godfrey Parker's new arrangement, called simply 'Craigielee'. Parker's 'Craigielee' had appeared once already in *The Colonial and Military Brass Band Journal* published by Thomas Bulch in Victoria. It's not a thing one could have heard in any other colony. The performance at Warrnambool races in 1894 could easily have been its world premiere.

Between Godfrey Parker's 'Craigielee' and James Barr's original tune the principal distinction is that the folkish old rhythm has been converted, to a quick march tempo—in 2:4 time.

Bulch (1860–1930) came to Australia in 1884 to escape the English weather. Settling first in Ballarat, he began a tireless project to advance the cause of band music in the homeland he had chosen. He opened music shops, taught students, ran bands and competitions, and published. He produced a great series of new tunes and arrangements, so the local bands would never lack fresh material to play.

Being so prolific, Bulch was afraid. If all his compositions were published in his name, bands and audiences might shy away and look elsewhere for variety. So he used a string of pseudonyms: Eugene Lacosti, Henry Lasker, Arthur Godfrey and so on. No one has traced a real Godfrey Parker; the name is almost certainly an alias for Bulch.

So on the list of creative sources of 'Waltzing Matilda' Bulch has earned a place. 'Craigielee' is not 'Waltzing Matilda' and parts of it aren't related at all. But the march tempo gives other parts a resemblance in rhythm and melody that James Barr's tune is lacking. Despite the obvious differences, a musician who compares the scores, where Chris Macpherson's tune is shown next to the relevant part of 'Craigielee', will see how her tune could indeed derive from a memory of the march she heard the year before.

Both tunes have similarities to 'The Bold Fusilier', but Chris Macpherson would not have had to know that song to arrive at her own.

So who could have put 'The Bold Fusilier' into 'Waltzing Matilda'? It's easy to overlook the fact that as she plucked her melody out she had a folksong expert standing at her shoulder. A man who spent time gathering traditional songs in the Australian bush just as folklorists and composers had been doing in Europe. Not a musician, but a man who understood poetic metres perfectly and knew how to pick them out of rhythms heard in songs. That was Banjo Paterson.

We're so used to his reputation as a poet, that all the other things he was are easily overlooked: horse racer, journalist, editor and lawyer; war correspondent and military officer, satirist, grazier and novelist. While Banjo was at Winton, some of these accomplishments still lay in his future. But back in 1895 he was already becoming the Australian authority on folk songs. His book, *Old Bush Songs,* published ten years later by Angus and Robertson, was the definitive collection till 1952. Songs from Aborigines, convicts and farming pioneers, gold diggers, drovers and all kinds of bushmen are printed together, in the versions he heard through the years. A lot of these songs he got from correspondents. In camps and in homesteads, in pubs and shearers' quarters, wherever his frequent travels led, he captured others as they were sung.

'Most of these songs,' he wrote in the introduction, 'even in the few years that they have been extant, have developed three or four different readings, and not only have the ballads been altered, but many of them have been forgotten altogether.'

The verses he published were composed in Australia, but it wasn't just Australian songs that were sung in the bush. 'The Bold Fusilier', if ever it was popular, is one of the songs that Banjo would have heard. When he set out to put words to Christina Macpherson's tune, its rhythmic similarity would have called the Fusilier up to his mind, at least semiconsciously, if not with awareness in full.

We can easily see how he might have been guided by the words of 'The Bold Fusilier':

BF: And he cried as he tramped through the drear streets of Rochester

WM: And he sang as he watched the old billy boiling

BF: Who'll be a sojer for Marlbro' with me?

WM: Who'll come a-waltzing Matilda with me?

This would be the first phase of a process that gave to 'Waltzing Matilda' the pattern and sound of 'The Bold Fusilier'.

There were three basic tunes for 'Waltzing Matilda', each of which has yielded its own crop of variants. The 1895 tune, Christina Macpherson's tune, carried the song in its first flush of popularity, in the inland of Queensland, in colonial times. To 'The Bold Fusilier' it has a slight resemblance, probably by accident. The words that were sung to it were Paterson's original or something very close. It's a tune that hardly anyone has heard.

Next was the 'Cloncurry' tune, also called the 'Buderim', which also is sung with the old form of words. It isn't like the others, it isn't like 'Craigielee' or 'The Bold Fusilier'. It dates from around the turn of the century. Almost everyone who hears it describes it as beautiful, and occasionally you'll still hear it played.

The 1903 tune worked out by Marie Cowan is essentially the one we're familiar with today. The words that are sung with it are as changed by Marie Cowan, and approved by Banjo Paterson in 1903. It was these words and music that the Inglis firm distributed to promote its Billy Tea.

Marie Cowan's husband was Inglis's manager in Sydney. The song back then was only just becoming known in New South Wales, but James Inglis was attracted by its reference to the singing swagman's boiling billy. The marketing strategy Inglis pursued stressed identification of the brand. His registered trademarks 100 years ago included depictions of a tea-drinking bushman, and a kangaroo who carried a billy and swag. In the twenty-first century, the Billy Tea packet carries part of the old branding, practically unchanged. Paterson knew

The tune known as the 'Cloncurry', 'Queensland' or 'Buderim' tune.

Inglis and probably supplied him with the words and the music he passed on to Marie Cowan.

One score she would have had was the simple, handwritten one that Banjo got for Inglis from Christina Macpherson. From these rough materials, she'd been asked to generate a version that was polished enough for amateurs to play, for tea drinkers to sing. If Marie Cowan knew of 'The Bold Fusilier', she recognised the clues to it in Paterson's words. She might have found an easy practical solution, modelling 'Waltzing Matilda' on 'The Bold Fusilier': '…he sang as he watched the old billy boiling', she made '…he sang as he watched and waited till his "Billy" boiled', a metrical match for '…he cried as he tramped through the drear streets of Rochester'.

So now we can pronounce on the swagman's state of jolliness—it was just to help 'Waltzing Matilda' sell tea.

To make the first line closer to the Fusilier metre, the adjective Marie Cowan wanted would have two syllables with the stress on the first. She could have had a 'sorry' swagman, but with tea to promote and a gay fusilier, he became 'jolly' instead. When her work was finished, the Waltzing Matilda words ran closely parallel to those of 'The Bold Fusilier'.

As for the melody, it looks as if she worked with scissors and paste on two different scores. Where

Marie Cowan's words and music in the Billy Tea leaflet, printed in Melbourne and published in Sydney, 1903.

one bar is lifted from Christina Macpherson's score, the next looks like a copy from 'The Bold Fusilier'. The hybrid tune she finished with scans with the lyrics, and sounds like the song as we know it today. Its grandmother is 'Craigielee', its mother is Chris Macpherson's melody. As for the father's identity, we admit it's not so easy to be sure, but readily suspect 'The Bold Fusilier'. Further back along our somewhat shaky pedigree are the eastern Europeans of the same paternal line.

One reason for uncertainty is that the oldest score we have for 'The Bold Fusilier' was first written down about 1962. By the time that it was written down, 'Waltzing Matilda' had been popular for decades, and no one knows what influence it had on the way people remember 'The Bold Fusilier'.

Musical historians, and Richard Magoffin, deny the antiquity of 'The Bold Fusilier'. To deal with their doubts and more musical details, we've added an appendix at the back of this book.

Now we can return to the problem that was posed at the start of the chapter. Is 'Waltzing Matilda' an Australian tune?

It certainly is. Most melodies in modern centuries resemble others, and most of them were influenced by others that existed before they were composed. No one can produce previous music, from Australia or elsewhere, the same as 'Waltzing

Matilda'—at most there are resemblances and works that are similar. The creative chain is there to trace forwards from 1805, when James Barr composed in Scotland. Thence it leads to Thomas Bulch, the Englishman in Victoria; via Warrnambool, to Chris Macpherson, a Victorian in Queensland, and Banjo, her collaborator, from New South Wales, who may have borrowed just a little from 'The Bold Fusilier'; and finally to another New South Welshman, Marie Cowan, in 1903. Each of these people made a creative contribution—they weren't just transmitting a pre-existing music.

There was scope for improvement in Marie Cowan's work. Over the years amendments have upgraded it, and new arrangements have multiplied, with many yet to come. Though the overwhelming majority are of the 'Cowan' family, quite a few are related to the 'Cloncurry' tune. As for the haunting and whimsical melody that 'Waltzing Matilda' was sung to in 1895, it is all but extinct and perhaps most Australians will never hear it played.

FROM THE BILLABONG TO THE WORLD

IN 1900, WHEN THE GOVERNOR OF QUEENS-
land requested 'Waltzing Matilda' at the Post Office
Hotel, it was already renowned beyond Winton, as
the distinctive tune of a remote locality.

When 'Waltzing Matilda' was beamed to Earth
from the space shuttle *Columbia* in the 1980s, it
certainly stood for more than that. Without even a
promotion campaign it had spread across boundaries of time and space to carry the swagman's cryptic message around the world and to every
succeeding generation.

Although the words were by a New South
Welshman, and the music by a Victorian, before
Federation it was a Queenslanders' song. To get
across state boundaries and into the minds of
people in all parts of Australia, it had to go to South
Africa first.

In October 1899 the first contingent of over 3000 Queenslanders, who would fight for Queen Victoria against the Boers, set off for South Africa to join men from all the other colonies. The Australians performed admirably, but it was an ugly, slow, messy war, which Britain finally won by weight of numbers. At home, the *Bulletin* writers railed against British imperialism. Banjo travelled on the same ship as the first Queenslanders, to cover the fighting as correspondent for the *Sydney Morning Herald* and the Melbourne *Argus*. Ultimately though, he joined the anti-war chorus. And perhaps he heard his song while he was there.

One of the Queenslanders reported a concert at which they performed 'Waltzing Matilda' to an audience including English soldiers (see Appendix I).

So after the war men who'd heard 'Waltzing Matilda' brought it back to their own states. It was sung in Sydney, where the Billy Tea Co.'s proprietor, James Inglis, was an amateur chorister, an opportunistic marketer and a friend of Banjo Paterson. In 1901 he had published a book, *A History of the Tea Trade*. In 1902 Banjo wrote to Chris Macpherson and got her to send a copy of the music for his musical friend.

In 1903 Marie Cowan, wife of one of Inglis's directors, wound up with the job of turning 'Waltzing Matilda' into a piece that would sell tea. Barely eight years old, the song had reached the main turning point in its career. Despite the fact that everyone has an individual version of the words, they almost all originate from Marie Cowan's revision, and her music supplies the usual tune.

Born in Bega, New South Wales, Marie is said to have been fond of Scottish songs, and her husband was Scottish born. Two scholars at least, John Manifold and Therese Radic, have speculated that she might therefore have known the 'Craigielee' music already. This is doubtful, because her music shows virtually no influence from the old Scottish tune, and there is no evidence of the later Victorian 'Craigielee' in New South Wales.

What materials she actually had to work with is considered in the previous chapter and Appendix I—without reaching the answer. How she went about it is equally unknown, but in *Who Wrote the Ballads?* (1964) John Manifold has a fictionalised reconstruction. He thought of Messrs Inglis and Cowan mucking around ineffectually at the office, trying to make good advertising material out of Banjo's song. Then Mr Cowan comes home from work to an inquisitive wife:

MR. 'You'd never guess what a strange job I have had to do today. Arranging for a

musical setting if you please, to a poem
about boiling a billy!'

MRS. 'How very odd! Is it for an
advertisement? What is the name of the
poem?'

MR. 'Oh, it's just a jingle as far as I can see;
not the sort of thing a really good musician
would want to touch. How does it run?
Heavens, I ought to know the ridiculous
thing by heart, I've been at it so long! Oh
yes, it's called "Waltzing Matilda".'

Fortunately for Australia, Marie takes charge—
pointing out that she should have been asked to
start with—and quickly sets the words to ideal
music. 'Marie, you're a genius!' declares her relieved
husband.

MRS. 'Oh, William, you are absurd! Why
that's just an old song I picked up in the
holidays, years ago before we met.'

MR. 'Marie, you are far too modest. That is
an admirable tune. Mr Inglis will be
delighted. Would you let me have a copy
before I leave for the Office tomorrow?
Naturally I shall see to it that you receive

due credit. No, no, don't protest! Of course you deserve the credit. Why, darling, you have solved the firm's advertising problem.'

MRS. 'Well, William, I know you will overbear me, but if my name appears, let it be only as arranger. It's an old song I learnt long ago...'

Next day Manifold has Cowan overbearing the boss as well, with the new arrangement, till Inglis concedes: 'Well, send this down to the printers. We'll put Billy Tea onto every cottage piano in the country, eh?' (p. 126).

Perhaps it did happen that quickly and accidentally, but maybe Marie had to work quite hard on it. She changed the words to fit the rhythm of her tune, and to repeat 'Billy' in the chorus by removing the mention of a waterbag. 'Billy' was given quote marks and a capital B to help with brand identification. Robyn Holmes, the National Library's Curator of Music, believes Marie might have had the help of a proper music publisher to polish up her work.

Her music and words were printed in Melbourne in large quantities by Allan and Co., the music printer and publisher. They were then distributed far and wide with Billy Tea.

The Australasian Students' Song Book, compiled in 1910, included 'Waltzing Matilda' in Marie

Cowan's version, introducing the bush song to new urban audiences.

The cultural boundary between the bush and the city was one of the biggest that 'Waltzing Matilda' had to cross. In those days native Australian culture was bush oriented; even if urban audiences were larger, inspiration came overwhelmingly from the bush, revelling in the Australian experience outside the city and suburbs.

Many of the *Bulletin* writers lived and worked in Sydney, but it was not their spiritual home, and most of the experiences they wrote about were from further out—the further out the better.

To this day the country and the outback take a part in Australian creativity—as sources of inspiration, gifted creators and attitudes—out of all proportion to the tediously statistical reference of head counts. Residents of suburbs who contemplate the matter generally accept as fact that despite their numerical prevalence, their experience is not quite the real thing; their freestanding homes on blocks of land are compromised replicas of country life. In art, literature, song and the very idea of life, the city is the poor cousin in Australia.

But in the 1890s and after, writers, including Banjo, came to acknowledge that there was an authentically Australian character type in the capital cities who could not be found anywhere else.

This was the larrikin of the inner suburbs—the antithesis of the noble bushman celebrated by Paterson and a stack of other poets. The larrikin was hard to warm to—mean and thuggish, narrow minded, short in conversation, unattractive in manners, generally weedy in build, lacking in aspiration and happiest as one of the push rather than as an individual.

Despite all that, this urban type gathered a literature around him. In a chapter of *An Outback Marriage*, Paterson's bushman is outmanoeuvred by larrikins. Louis Stone's novel *Jonah* is a story of a Sydney push with inhumane heroes.

The ultimate development of this movement comes from C. J. Dennis—dubbed 'the laureate of the larrikin'—famous creator of *The Sentimental Bloke*. Writing before, during and after World War I, Dennis sympathetically depicts an inner-Melbourne populace totally indifferent to the bush and the Australian culture that comes from it: yet itself distinctively Australian, as if to contradict the generally accepted notions of authenticity.

In *The Moods of Ginger Mick* (1916) one of Dennis's larrikins goes to fight with the Anzacs. He makes the amazing discovery that city or country, rich or poor, one state or another, all the Australians have more in common with each other than anyone else.

There is farmers frum the Mallee, there is
    bushmen down frum Bourke,
There's college men wiv letters to their name,
There is grafters an there's blokes 'oo never
    done a 'ard day's work
Till they tumbled, wiv the rest, into the
    game—
An' they're drillin; 'ere together, men uv ev'ry
    creed an kind.
It's Australia! Solid! Dinkum! That 'as left
    the land be'ind.

'The Push'

In one of the Ginger Mick poems, 'The Singing
Soldiers', Mick comments from Gallipoli on the
way the Australian troops had of singing all the
time, and lists many of their favourite songs. In a
significant demonstration of the inner-city perspective, the songs are from overseas—no old bush
songs from Australia among them. There is just one
exception as the second-last verse reveals:

'When I'm sittin' in me dug out wiv the bul-
    lets droppin' near,'
Writes ole Ginger; 'an' a chorus smacks me
    in the flamin' ear;
P'raps a song that Rickards billed, er p'raps
    a line o' "Waltz Matilder",

Then I feel I'm in Australia, took an shifted
   over 'ere.'

This is the first published reference to 'Waltzing Matilda' by a major writer, and proves that in
1915 it had penetrated the hard shell of the city
dweller.

In 1917 *Saltbush Bill and Other Verses* was a new
collection of Paterson poems, in a pocket edition with
the troops in mind. It included 'Waltzing Matilda'—
the first time that Banjo's old Queensland version of
the words was printed and distributed in large numbers. In 1918 'Waltzing Matilda' was included in a
special songbook published for servicemen.

The Boer War and both World Wars helped
a great deal in promoting 'Waltzing Matilda',
because when a few men who knew it began to
sing, the result was that every man in the squad
knew it when they'd finished. Returning to Australia, veterans helped make it known all over the
country.

Between the World Wars, the first recordings
were made, and the song was heard on the radio.
In the early 1930s a senior British musician,
Thomas Wood, visited Australia and reached the
conclusion that 'Waltzing Matilda' was Australia's
only genuine folk song. He made an effort to track

the music down; and found it eventually in a convent in Queensland.

He worked to improve the score, and included it with the words in his travel book, *Cobbers,* published in London in 1934. *Cobbers* was a huge success, running through sixteen print runs, and for the first time familiarising overseas readers with the song.

As the generations marched on, the song's significance was changing. Its quaint phraseology even at the start meant that it was not an expression in vernacular Australian. But because only Australians knew what the words mean, it became a kind of coded message, signifying their complicity with one another in an uncomprehending world. This undoubtedly encouraged its use in theatres of war as a defiant gesture of identity to allies and enemies. So a bush yarn with fancy terminology naturally became the emblematic national song.

The tragic defiance of the underdog in the song helped the process along by identifying Australians to themselves and others as a people who did not meekly swallow the simplistic notions of the rest of the Western world concerning such matters. The song still struck many as a political protest as well, but the political interpretation had been detached from the labour troubles of the 1890s to become more abstract, as even Richard Magoffin concedes, in *Fair Dinkum Matilda*:

> In 1895 the song must have seemed a plea
> that the spirit of the swagman should not be
> allowed to perish; in 1939 it would be seen
> as an affirmation that the spirit of the
> swagman had survived. (p. 35)

During World War II Australian servicemen sang it in preference to any other song. In 1941, for instance, the international press reported that they sang it in North Africa when they entered Bardia, a fortification that vastly outnumbering Italians could not hold.

In his country residence, at a meeting with Robert Menzies and Charles de Gaulle, Britain's Prime Minister Winston Churchill sang 'Waltzing Matilda', and is said to have remarked 'That's one of the finest songs in the world'.

Banjo Paterson died during World War II, and people started writing about the provenance of his song. The author Sydney May entered 'Waltzing Matilda' into the elite and tiny company of songs that have had whole books written about them. Books were still being written about it until at least 2006.

It became a fashion in naming. In 1942 a new class of British tanks was called the Waltzing Matilda. One of the Halifax bombers used in air raids against Europe was *Waltzing Matilda* as was an American B-29, built to bomb Japan, that visited Australian country areas. After the War the naming penchant continued on more benign articles such as yachts and passenger aircraft.

The song came home in jubilant style after the War, to a country that embraced it fervently, and it enjoyed universal endorsement in a grateful peacetime era. Primary schools that had earnestly sung 'There'll Always be an England' dropped that and took up 'Waltzing Matilda'.

Saturating popular culture since the War, 'Waltzing Matilda' has buried itself deep in our lore and literature. 'Waltzing Matilda and Banjo Paterson together surely are the foundation of all Australian songs and music,' remarked the singer and songwriter John Williamson. 'Waltzing Matilda stirs the heart deep within the ordinary Australian. Whether Banjo intended it or not I believe it is the classic battler's anthem.'

Sometimes it finds its way overtly into other pieces of music, such as 'And the Band Played Waltzing Matilda', Eric Bogle's modern ballad of a bushman and Gallipoli veteran:

From the Murray's green basin to the dusty
     outback,
Well I waltzed my Matilda all over.

The song tells his melancholy story of a crip-
pling injury, 'Waltzing Matilda' lending piquancy
in each progressive chorus—

And the band played 'Waltzing Matilda',
As they carried us down the gangway,
But nobody cheered, they just stood there
     and stared,
Then they turned their faces away.

In a similar way, the song crops up repeatedly
in art, film and literature, sometimes as mere background, sometimes playing a significant role. Nigel
Krauth's 1983 novel *Matilda, My Darling* is loosely
based on circumstances surrounding the invention
of the song. It supplies the words to children's pic-
ture books, takes a prominent place on soundtracks
and is the subject of a play and short films, including one with puppet animation.

The huge number of recordings has helped
make the song instantly recognisable in many parts
of the world. The best estimate is that there
have been over 600 distinct recordings made of

'Waltzing Matilda' since the first on record, produced in 1927 by John Collinson and sung by an
anonymous Queensland tenor. The deep baritone
rendition in Peter Dawson's wartime record proved
very effective in Australia and overseas at spread-
ing the song into ordinary homes. Harry Belafonte's
version popularised 'Waltzing Matilda' on the
American market.

Most recordings are in folk-music styles, with
a few in a somewhat Americanised 'country' style.
The version carried on the space shuttle was sung
by the late Slim Dusty. 'I remember how proud
I was to know that my version of "Waltzing
Matilda" was beamed to Earth as the astronauts
Crippen and Young passed over Australia,' he
commented. 'I remember thinking they couldn't
have chosen any better song to greet and pay their
respects to Australia.'

The song lends itself well to different languages
and music styles and several rock musicians have
taken it on, including Bill Haley in 1958 and David
Evans in 1986.

There are always new recordings: 2006 brought
the Mills sisters, with their enchanting translation
into a Northern Territory Aboriginal hybrid dialect.
While the word billabong goes unaltered into their
dialect, 'ghost' has to become 'spirit', and 'jumbuck'

from the southern Aborigines is simply replaced with the sound 'ba-aa'.

There are dozens of more or less successful translations, including at least one into Latin, which is perhaps waiting for a suitable recording artist:

> Olim sedebat prope ripam fluminis
> Solus grassator sub umbra fagi,
> Et cantabat homo dum aestuaret cortina,
> Veni et saltemus Matilda, veni!

Naturally large sums have changed hands over 'Waltzing Matilda', especially to secure rights to use it in records, movies, reprints and live performances. It's an ironic demonstration of what a failure our intellectual property laws are in their original intention of rewarding the labours of creative people. Some people have made large sums from 'Waltzing Matilda'. But Banjo remarked that all he got for it was 'a few bob'. Christina Macpherson and Thomas Bulch, who could both have used the money, never saw a brass razoo from it. It is not known whether Marie Cowan benefited; she is thought to have promised any earnings to charity.

Each new arrangement attracts a new copyright—which used to create a monopoly lasting till 50 years after the arranging 'author's' death or

50 years after posthumous publication. This extremely long period is no use to the creator, but even now it hampers people from making legitimate use of 'Waltzing Matilda' and a million other musical, artistic and literary relics. The advantage accrues to vested business interests that have generally acquired rights for a pittance and go on exploiting them and obstructing users for as long as the law allows.

Recently, thanks to the 'American Free Trade Agreement' the term of these posthumous monopolies in Australia has been increased to 70 years, for the purpose of granting a windfall to certain large US companies that control rights in internationally valuable properties. The aim was not to restrict the access Australians have to their own culture—that is just an accidental result of government policy. If a 20 year old in 2007 publishes a new arrangement of 'Waltzing Matilda', and then lives to the age of seventy, the new version will not enter the public domain until the year 2128.

Live performances of 'Waltzing Matilda' have reached larger audiences than most songs, and been relayed internationally, because it is routinely played and sung at sporting events. In the MCG in 1956 massed choirs at the Olympic Games closing ceremony sang it to its first global TV, film and radio audience, as well as to the packed grandstands. In a later century, the International Rugby Board thought it could defy this enthusiasm for 'Waltzing Matilda'. From its headquarters in Ireland the Board prohibited 'Waltzing Matilda' at matches in the 2003 World Cup. The Board allowed official national anthems, but otherwise only performances of 'cultural significance' such as New Zealand's haka. The claim that 'Waltzing Matilda' is not culturally significant to Australians was like a red rag to a bull: indignant politicians, sportspeople, community leaders and journalists unleashed a torrent of protest. The Board must have realised that its decree had no power to prevent crowds from singing the subversive song at the top of their throats, and it reluctantly backed down. Rarely has it been sung so defiantly and loud by such large numbers as at the World Cup games that year. Perhaps the Board will not repeat its mistake.

Australians, it turns out, are not the only people who can sing it en masse. In 1993 when former Prime Minister Paul Keating went to the Gaelic football grand final at Croke Park in Dublin, the whole Irish crowd sang 'Waltzing Matilda'. 'Afterwards I was aware of the extraordinary power of this song on an Australian's senses, he remarked.

All sorts of music can move us, but to hear 'Waltzing Matilda' sung so fervently and beautifully by the people of another country 12,000 miles from home is to know that nothing can move us like our own song.

Keating made these remarks in a 1995 speech at the North Gregory Hotel, at celebrations for the centenary of 'Waltzing Matilda'. Further up Elderslie Street, in 1998, the magnificent Waltzing Matilda Centre was opened. Part museum, part shrine, it showcases the song to visitors. Presumably somewhere else in the world you can find a building that exists to honour a particular song— but it's not usual and it's a mark of the singular status of 'Waltzing Matilda' in the world that we have such a building in Australia.

UP JUMPED THE EXPERTS

WHEN AN OLD PLAY OR POEM OR BOOK or song cements itself in a culture, experts arise to declare with firm assurance that the author who is famous for it is bogus.

Shakespeare could not have written the plays, they said, in an argument that raged for a hundred years in Britain. Experts stripped Confucius of the authorship of an old classic, *Spring and Autumn*, without the need of evidence. 'It's not the sort of book he would have written,' they decided. The *Iliad* and *Odyssey* of Homer are the foundation of Greek literature—of all Western literature really. Could Homer be left with the credit? Clearly not. Scholars still maintain that they are the joined up works of many anonymous creators, not quite consistent with each other.

A favourite argument against traditional claims of authorship is that one work is too unlike another to come from the same hand. So Christopher Brennan, most academic of the *Bulletin* poets, declared with flat authority that it is impossible that Homer gives us both the *Odyssey* and *Iliad*.

The *Iliad* is a unified tour de force, awe inspiring in its sustained intensity. Anyone who reads it as an inconsistent pastiche must be blind to its overarching genius—but such at times is the expert's way.

Brennan's claim that differing works must come from different authors is undermined by examples where authorship admits of no dispute. The poet C. J. Dennis comes to mind, who in Brennan's time wrote *The Sentimental Bloke* as well as *The Glugs of Gosh*: works far more unalike than Homer's epics are.

No one bothers about the authenticity of an ordinary song. But even when Banjo was alive, challenges to his claim to be the author of 'Waltzing Matilda' were in the air. In the 1930s Charles Fenner (1884–1955), author of *Bunyips and Billabongs* (1933), told Clement Semmler that Banjo Paterson might not have been the writer. Semmler, in *The Banjo of the Bush* (1966, p. 95), explains that Fenner wrongly thought a *Bulletin* cartoonist, D. H. Souter, had claimed 'Waltzing Matilda' as his own. E. J. Brady (1869–1952), another *Bulletin* balladist, said in a letter to Oscar Mendelsohn in November 1946: 'Banjo never wrote it at all. It used to be sung in the bush when I was a boy…Look up the matter further and find where Paterson ever claimed to be the author of "Waltzing Matilda"'.

The idea that Banjo simply improved a folk song that had long been in existence was supported in 1956 by Professor Russell Ward. In his article 'Waltzing Matilda', Ward's point was that 'Waltzing Matilda' is unlike everything else that Banjo wrote and could not therefore be his. Ward encouraged the idea that an old Waltzing Matilda folk song had existed, perhaps in the upper Murrumbidgee of Paterson's childhood. Paterson had collected all the old bush songs he could lay hands on, for his anthology *Old Bush Songs*. He could have held 'Waltzing Matilda' back from its rightful place and taken credit for the lyrics.

The old bush version became a sort of grail that people spoke of but couldn't find.

The chapter 'Centuries in the Making' considered the theory of Harry Pearce about German origins of 'Waltzing Matilda'. In *On the Origins of Waltzing Matilda* published in 1971, Pearce insisted that the existence of 'Waltzing Matilda' could only be explained by some intermediate Australian stage between its European forerunner and the popular version. What could this be, he asked, other than 'the old bush song', conjured into existence to fill the void left by his inability to conceive of the creative process that might have drawn something new out of Banjo, Chris Macpherson and Marie Cowan.

It didn't help these revisionist theories that no one could find any traces of the old bush version except in recollections claimed by a few old timers such as E. J. Brady, mostly from the Riverina and upper Murrumbidgee. The only old song resembling 'Waltzing Matilda' was 'The Bold Fusilier', completely un-Australian in subject matter, which no one could establish was sung in Banjo's youth.

While the Banjo deniers were writing letters, articles and books, another school was defending what in hindsight was the orthodox position. Sydney May with his 1944 book *The Story of Waltzing Matilda* presented cogent evidence of the circumstances in which Banjo and Chris begat 'Waltzing Matilda'. Even without May's research it was easy to answer Brady's challenge 'find where Paterson ever claimed to be the author'. For one thing, 'Waltzing Matilda' appears in Paterson's 1917 book *Saltbush Bill and other Verses*.

Banjo's express claim to the words obliged the deniers to accuse him of dishonesty. As Paterson's biographer, Clement Semmler, points out, Banjo is renowned for being honest, upright and modest; that he lied was an audacious claim, and would take a lot of proving. One of the deniers, Oscar Mendelsohn, admitted what they were up against: 'I suppose the riddle will never be solved why so upright a man as Andrew Barton Paterson could have failed to tell the world, if it was a fact, that he had not written but had merely doctored "Waltzing Matilda"'.

Who Wrote the Ballads? by the poet and music historian J. S. Manifold came out in 1964. Manifold came from one of the wealthiest Victorian squatter families, with stations in the Western District near Camperdown and Warrnambool. They also had a share in Sesbania station near Dagworth, where his father learnt 'Waltzing Matilda' by ear. Manifold had no time for the doubters and gave the orthodox account as definitive. Semmler's *Banjo of the Bush* came out in 1966, with a revised edition in 1974. His chapter VIII includes an eloquent rebuttal of the challenge to Banjo's authorship.

The point made by Ward and his followers— that 'Waltzing Matilda' differs in style and structure from all his other writing—was easily discarded by Semmler's observation that only 'Waltzing Matilda' was written to music. One of the doubters, A. A. Phillips, had already recanted on this basis: 'I had forgotten that, according to the story, Paterson wrote the words of "Waltzing Matilda" to fit an already chosen tune.'

Behind the scenes, while these works were being published, Richard Magoffin from Quambetook near Dagworth was assiduously gathering all the extant evidence from official records and persons with memories of the old days. He built up a thorough account of the people and times, which except in finer detail supported the versions of Manifold and May. In a voluminous correspondence, Magoffin tried to deflect Harry Pearce and persuade him of the orthodox account. But the old man stuck to his guns. Magoffin's own book *Fair Dinkum Matilda* came out in 1973, two years after Pearce's, and ever since, Pearce's 'Old Bush Song' has been ignored.

Perhaps when experts challenge traditional claims to authorship, they sometimes have right on their side, or at least a workable case. But the case against Banjo Paterson was untenable from the start. The one thing it proved was the importance of the song—because people could misdirect so much time and ingenuity on a fairly simple issue.

Meanwhile one of the deniers had opened up the battle on a new front. Oscar Mendelsohn was one of those who claimed that Banjo plagiarised a folk song collected for his *Old Bush Songs* anthology. In his 1966 book, *A Waltz with Matilda*, Mendelsohn included a more unusual claim: that the music was composed by Harry Nathan. Like Charles Mackerras, Nathan was a musically gifted descendant of famous colonial musician, Isaac Nathan. He'd been a cathedral organist in Townsville but finished up an alcoholic, in Toowoomba.

Mendelsohn relied on a copy in Sydney's Mitchell Library of a fairly sophisticated arrangement of 'Waltzing Matilda' melodically similar to Marie Cowan's, written in Nathan's hand. It was the oldest manuscript of 'Waltzing Matilda' music then known, and an impressive piece of evidence. But after Richard Magoffin flushed out Chris Macpherson's manuscripts of the 1895 version, Mendelsohn ceased to find adherents.

Harry Nathan staged a surprise comeback in 1996 when the *Journal of Australian Studies* published 'The Songlines of Waltzing Matilda' by Therese Radic, a university academic in Melbourne. 'Arguments have been brought that he was once the book-keeper at Dagworth,' she writes of Nathan. 'It is said that he helped Christina with her attempts to cut *Waltzing Matilda* into the paper rolls of the harmonium-like instrument at Dagworth, she having acquired her known skill at this from him.'

This is odd. Mendelsohn did not say that Nathan went to Dagworth—let alone that he helped Christina. Therese Radic doesn't indicate where 'the arguments' were brought, but the Dagworth book-keeper, J. T. Wilson, may have been on leave when the song was written. Magoffin discovered from station records that Wilson was replaced while on leave by a man named Drysdale.

Given the words she used, it seems unlikely that Dr Radic has an undeclared primary source putting Nathan in the right time and place to be involved. He can probably be dismissed from the scene. But not from the story completely. His work and Marie Cowan's are so alike that one must have copied the other, or both have drawn on a common source. The implications are considered in Appendix I.

Therese Radic brings a refreshing perspective to the Waltzing Matilda dialogue in the form of scathingly negative opinions about people and things that are normally admired. She starts on the scholars who preceded her:

> Each rubbishes his predecessor in an attempt
> to claim the territory of origin. Claim *this*
> territory and you position yourself to claim
> the right to act as singer-up of the ancestor's
> power. This is Richard Magoffin's stance. By
> subsuming his sometimes unacknowledged

predecessors' evidence and outliving most of
them, he has become the sole interpreter of
the song and keeper of a sacred site he keeps
shifting.

Journal of Australian Studies, vol. 49, p. 40

This is hard on Magoffin, whose position was fairly stable and who repeatedly acknowledged his predecessors. Dr Radic has a similarly dim view of those who played a creative role. Josephine Pene was 'known as a pianist and no lady'. Marie Cowan's music was 'schoolgirlish'. Banjo had been 'racketing about the district with the males of the family and their retainers' (odd, because the only extant reminiscences have him travelling in mixed company in a relatively genteel buggy).

Supporters of 'Waltzing Matilda' depressed her—a tea merchant, 'the great Australian god of sport', 'what passed for the gentry', 'the leftist intellectuals of the folk music revival', earnest nationalists, radio chat shows et al. She lamented that the song would be a ready tool for those who would harness it, 'God help us all', for the Sydney Olympics and the Centenary of Federation.

Conceived by a lawyer-poet and a squatter's daughter, drawing on the resources of the

male cult of bush poetry crafted largely by
urbanised idealists, vaguely remembered
Scottish parlour-songs and Presbyterian
hymns, it came into existence as an
expression of middle class migrant nostalgia.
It had no right to live…

Journal of Australian Studies, vol. 49, p. 45

It's an interesting question: who should judge
whether a song has the right to live? Some will perhaps condemn the jaundiced view of Therese
Radic—but in fact she is the eloquent voice of the
unnumbered and otherwise inarticulate people for
whom 'Waltzing Matilda' and everything that goes
with it are regrettable.

It's salutary to notice, in the midst of celebrat-
ing something that seems to join disparate people
in glad consensus, that some still can't participate—
acceptance of that is a lesson in acceptance of the
diversity of humankind.

We can't assume that the jolly swagman would
have been upset by her despairing attitude; he might
well have recognised her as a long-lost sister.

In the matter of scholarship unfortunately,
Therese Radic is less impressive. Her little article is
riddled with careless errors of detail, which seem to
spring from a disregard of sources and a preference

for prejudice over evidence. However strong she might be in her field of expertise, in the study of 'Waltzing Matilda' she was a lightweight, whose account had been best ignored. That's not what happened.

Dr Radic was a historical adviser for the displays in the Waltzing Matilda Centre, opened by the Shire of Winton in 1998. Richard Magoffin, despite being a local, and the leading expert, and having agitated insistently for the state government funding it ultimately received, was not involved.

The exclusion he seems to have taken calmly enough, but when the Centre opened he objected vehemently to historical errors in the presentation, to what he saw as injustice to people who were defamed, including Josephine Pene, and to its neglect of Christina Macpherson. In Kynuna he set up Matilda Expo, advertising for visitors the chance to get 'the real story', and performing the song with the original words, to Chris Macpherson's tune, which is unknown in Winton. Visitors to the district found Winton and Kynuna locked in a tussle, each offering a different Waltzing Matilda experience, like religious centres of opposing faiths.

The situation has changed. In 2005, poor health obliged Magoffin to abandon Matilda Expo, and his collection of research papers has gone to the

National Library in Canberra. The Waltzing Matilda Centre has been moving to a more open-minded and conscientious approach, so the opposition is no longer evident. It's a pity for the Centre that its earlier intransigence caused it to miss out on the fundamental archive, though in Canberra Magoffin's papers are more accessible to most Australians.

The Waltzing Matilda Centre has overcome the old historical anomalies of its presentation. It does not present specific interpretations, including the political interpretation based on Magoffin's allegorical analysis. Though Therese Radic didn't contest the political reading, she thought of it as men's business, and clearly it annoyed her. That may be why it got no look in at Winton to begin with, but Winton has since found a scholarly rejoinder to the political reading.

Vision Splendid (2004), the Council's beautifully written and produced book on the history of the Winton district, is an example for other towns. But the book's authors Peter and Sheila Forrest open their study of 'Waltzing Matilda' with the following manifestly false observation: 'Until quite recently, a conventional account could have been given about the origins of *Waltzing Matilda* without much risk of starting an argument.' (p. 93).

They review evidence and theories, including Magoffin's proposition that Banjo helped to settle the union dispute—which they consider most unlikely. Unfortunately their conclusion is partly based on the observation that if Paterson had a central role, others would have written about it because he was so prominent ('a celebrity'). At the time though, Bartie Paterson, as he was known personally, was nobody to the Queensland public. Only when his first book was published would the world learn that the famous Banjo was A. B. Paterson.

The Forrests deny that Frenchy Hoffmeister was the inspiration for Banjo's swagman. They point to Frenchy's hostility to the squatters (Banjo's friends), his advocacy of violence and dodging of the law: 'Not a man likely to have captured Banjo's sympathetic imagination, we think' (p. 104).

In this they misjudge the poet who in 1894 wrote 'How Gilbert Died' (sympathetically treating a bushranger who plundered districts where Banjo's family had stations); and who in 'Father Riley's Horse' would show 'the horse thief Andy Regan' in a positive light.

The Forrests make no mention of the allegorical reading but it is likely that they reject it. After reviewing much of the available information they come to this opinion: 'We do not think that Paterson wrote the poem about any one incident or series of events' (p. 105).

At least since Mendelsohn's time, people have been opposing the interpretation of 'Waltzing Matilda' as a political protest or allegory. But as no one has succeeded in undermining the political reading, Magoffin's followers will probably not give it up, but rather recruit new fellows. Now that the challenges to the authorship of Banjo and Chris Macpherson are defeated, the song's political and socio-economic significance is the most controversial thing about it.

But one thing we can count on is that conflicts won't end there. So far the song is virtually untouched by academic theorists.

But as they are increasingly crowded out by closer settlement, they must make their way over the horizon to squat on newer pastures.

See how their old Marxism run was fenced in by selectors and overstocked to penury; and how far the theorists had to drive their herds to find long grass in newer fields.

'Waltzing Matilda' is a nice little paddock with plenty of feed on it for the enterprising neo-feminist, post-structuralist or group functional inter-mutualist. Why are they waiting? Foucault showed them long ago how to survey the land. It could all be fenced in on the principles of Lucy Rigaray, and with a Lacanian bore on the place it could be practically drought proof. The boundary disputes alone will give them something rewarding to do in their universities for years to come. Imagine how fat their jumbucks will get, and the quantities of superfine wool that will be produced.

The cynical reader may think this a jest. But it is a fact that universities have hardly begun on 'Waltzing Matilda'. In this chapter only two university academics are identified as contributors to the controversies, in both cases retarding the cause of knowledge.

The trustworthy knowledge we have now of 'Waltzing Matilda' and its origins is all the work of poets, school teachers, graziers, a librarian and a broadcaster. Fortunately they came forward and did the work and the PhDs held back—now we have common sense and understanding rather than a distorted university mythology.

The fact that universities do not contribute to our little subject does not detract from their indispensable importance. Even the theoretical exponents of the human sciences, who seem to the laity to offer nothing of worth, have a part to play. Think of monasteries on the eve of the Renaissance. The progress of the mind and spirit that would soon take place outside their cloisters depended on the work of their inmates. All the scholastic incantations and rules, their ornate and baffling elaborations from scripture, seemed pointless in a clearer light. But the tools of learning they cultivated, the texts they preserved without understanding—were essential resources in the forthcoming project of enlightenment and inspiration. So today, if capable scholars, without the academic handicaps, are going to foster culture and thought, they will need the assets that academics have garnered, even as they undermine the academic bulwark of prejudice and mumbo jumbo.

HOW GILBERT DIED

There's never a stone at the sleeper's head,
    There's never a fence beside,
And the wandering stock on the grave may tread
    Unnoticed and undenied,
But the smallest child on the Watershed
    Can tell you how Gilbert died.

For he rode at dusk, with his comrade Dunn
    To the hut at the Stockman's Ford,
In the waning light of the sinking sun
    They peered with a fierce accord.
They were outlaws both—and on each man's head
    Was a thousand pounds reward.

They had taken toll of the country round,
    And the troopers came behind
With a black that tracked like a human hound
    In the scrub and the ranges blind:
He could run the trail where a white man's eye
    No sign of a track could find.

He had hunted them out of the One Tree Hill
    And over the Old Man Plain,
But they wheeled their tracks with a wild beast's skill,
    And they made for the range again.
Then away to the hut where their grandsire dwelt,
    They rode with a loosened rain.

And their grandsire gave them a greeting bold:
    'Come in and rest in peace,

No safer place does the country hold—
　　With the night pursuit must cease,
And we'll drink success to the roving boys,
　　And to hell with the black police.'

But they went to death when they entered there,
　　In the hut at the Stockman's Ford,
For their grandsire's words were as false as fair—
　　They were doomed to the hangman's cord.
He had sold them both to the black police
　　For the sake of the big reward.

In the depth of night there are forms that glide
　　As stealthy as serpents creep,
And around the hut where the outlaws hide
　　They plant in the shadows deep,
And they wait till the first faint flush of dawn
　　Shall waken their prey from sleep.

But Gilbert wakes while the night is dark—
　　A restless sleeper, aye,
He has heard the sound of a sheepdog's bark,
　　And his horse's warning neigh,
And he says to his mate, 'There are hawks abroad,
　　And it's time that we went away.'

Their rifles stood at the stretcher head,
　　Their bridles lay to hand,
They wakened the old man out of his bed,
　　When they heard the sharp command:
'In the name of the Queen lay down your arms,
　　Now, Dunn and Gilbert, stand!'

Then Gilbert reached for his rifle true
    That close at his hand he kept,
He pointed it straight at the voice and drew,
    But never a flash outleapt,
For the water ran from the rifle breach—
    It was drenched while the outlaws slept.

Then he dropped the piece with a bitter oath,
    And he turned to his comrade Dunn:
'We are sold,' he said, 'we are dead men both,
    But there may be a chance for one;
I'll stop and I'll fight with the pistol here,
    You take to your heels and run.'

So Dunn crept out on his hands and knees
    In the dim, half-dawning light,
And he made his way to a patch of trees,
    And vanished among the night,
And the trackers hunted his tracks all day,
    But they never could trace his flight.

But Gilbert walked from the open door
    In a confident style and rash:
He heard at his side the rifles roar,
    And he heard the bullets crash.
But he laughed as he lifted his pistol-hand,
    And he fired at the rifle flash.

Then out of the shadows the troopers aimed
    At his voice and the pistol sound,
With the rifle flashes the darkness flamed,
    He staggered and spun around,

And they riddled his body with rifle balls
    As it lay on the blood-soaked ground.

There's never a stone at the sleeper's head
    There's never a fence beside,
And the wandering stock on the grave may tread
    Unnoticed and undenied,
But the smallest child on the Watershed
    Can tell you how Gilbert died.

Vol. I, p. 215

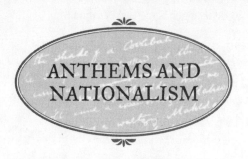

ANTHEMS AND NATIONALISM

IN HELSINKI IN 1952 the strains of 'Waltzing Matilda' flooded the Olympic Stadium as sprinter Marjorie Jackson stood on the winner's podium with a gold medal hanging from her neck. Australian officials went into a flurry. 'Waltzing Matilda' was a mistake, and they insisted on 'God Save the Queen'. Games organisers explained that they believed 'Waltzing Matilda' to be Australia's national song—a misapprehension shared with many people overseas.

If anyone had said to Banjo at Dagworth, or to Marie Cowan as she worked on her Billy Tea project, that their words would be sung on state occasions to express official patriotism, they would have laughed. But after World War II, for as long as Australia had only 'God Save the Queen' and no anthem of its own, 'Waltzing Matilda' was muddled up in debates and confusions about anthem status. In the Northern Hemisphere, on sheet music and recordings, it was routinely billed as 'Australia's unofficial national anthem'.

'Waltzing Matilda' was put forward in the 1970s' votes and policy changes on which tune and song should become the national anthem, despite having none of the declarations of national pride, freedom, superiority or loyal devotion expected in national anthems. It appealed to the cynicism, irony and dry humour of Australians to think of it as an anthem. In the 1977 plebiscite, it polled second in a field of four:

'Advance Australia Fair'	2 940 854	votes
'Waltzing Matilda'	1 918 206	
'God Save the Queen'	1 257 341	
'Song of Australia'	652 858.	

Some commentators suggested that 'Waltzing Matilda' was most people's second choice, and that it would win a preferential ballot, such as members of parliament are selected by.

The whole issue was partly a question of how close Australia needed to be to other countries in the way it handles these considerations. Canada became an illustration of what might have been: despite its loyalty to the Queen it got an anthem,

'O Canada', which did not mention her, and a flag without the Union Jack on it, so that occasionally, when Canada claims world attention in its own right, it is equipped with unique emblems for the purpose.

In the corner of the Canadian classroom is a distinctive maple leaf flag. Each morning the pupils face the flag and swear a ponderous oath of loyalty to Canada. Then they sing in unison to the doleful strains of 'O Canada'.

They perform this daily ritual because they have learnt to do so from their neighbours in the USA, where this particular procedure for demonstrating patriotism was perfected. In their energetic efforts to declare themselves faithful Canadians, they repeatedly prove how American they are.

Something that distinguishes Australians from many foreigners is their disdain for patriotic demonstrations of that sort. Yet even Australians are sincerely patriotic. Two different kinds of patriotism are demonstrated in Australia.

One is serious, straightforward and strident. Its colours are blue, white and red. Its annual celebration is Australia Day; and its song is 'Advance Australia Fair'. It is promoted by certain political leaders and primary school teachers, by commercial sponsors and Federal Government initiatives. It is the same as patriotism overseas.

The other kind is sardonic, complicated, subtle and pervasive. Its colours are green and yellow. Its annual commemoration is Anzac Day. Its song is 'Waltzing Matilda'. It involves normal Australians being themselves and needs no promoters. It is uniquely Australian.

Requiring people to sing the national anthem is the most insistent activity of the first breed of patriotism. Apart from the very young and impressionable, those who sing it with most fervour are those whose Australianness is most marginal. Professional basketball players sing along eagerly when it is played at important matches. Footballers and cricketers don't even have to mouth the words.

'Advance Australia Fair' is the work of a Scotsman, P. D. McCormick, but it was in fact written in Australia. The only Australian thing about it is the constant reiteration of the name. Otherwise it is just the same as a stack of other jingoistic songs such as 'O Canada', 'Land of Hope and Glory' and 'God Help New Zealand'.

A quick survey of the first verse points up some difficulties that this presents:

Australians all let us rejoice
For we are young and free

The claim to be young can only be made for Australia the political entity—not for Australians, who have such a low birth rate that on average they are one of the world's oldest nations. With every passing hour Australia becomes more an old person's country—in thought, conduct and demography. The quality of being free is general throughout the world if you believe national anthems. In fact wherever you are, the celebrated freedom is heavily qualified—as the jolly swagman and those who tangle with copyright laws when they try to sing about him have discovered.

> We've golden soil and wealth for toil
> Our home is girt by sea.

In 1878 McCormick must have meant that there is a lot of gold to be mined in Australia. Now that it's all been dug up and sent overseas, it isn't something to keep singing about. Of course as the remaining minerals are dug up and sent away, and soil nutrients are permanently extracted by vast underpriced agricultural exports, the soil becomes more and more like desert sand each day, so 'golden soil' will again become appropriate. McCormick is urgent in his work ethic as 'wealth for toil' reveals. At least though, having a home with a moat around it, 'girt by sea', really is a matter for self-congratulation.

Our land abounds in Nature's gifts,
Of beauties rich and rare.

The concept of beauties that are both rare and abundant is the main difficulty in this pair of lines—but such are the exigencies of rhyme.

On History's page let every stage
Advance Australia fair.

The second verse is known to few people, so some highlights are selected below:

Beneath our radiant Southern Cross

The notion that we have some ownership in the Southern Cross, or even that it is a distinctive feature, is curious considering that it is visible from most of the Earth's surface. Its association with Australia and other southern lands was born in the minds of Northern Hemisphere navigators who used it to guide their imperialistic journeys. It's no more appropriate as an emblem for native residents than the Moon or any other visible constellation.

We'll toil with heart and hands

McCormick's enthusiasm for toil is such that he wants even our hearts hard at work.

For those who've come across the seas,
We've boundless plains to share

This popular error has caused endless bother. Federal legislation being introduced in 2006 provides that those who come across the seas will be denied admission, and incarcerated on a destitute Pacific island. Under the old more liberal regime we spare them a ten by ten cell in a desert camp.

The comments above are just ill-natured carping, which results from the jolt that comes from descending to 'Advance Australia Fair' after too much time with 'Waltzing Matilda'. In fact most Australians would agree that an anthem is necessary and 'Waltzing Matilda' is only a song for people to sing because they want to, not because it is a duty. Perhaps the answer is to strip 'Advance Australia Fair' of the more absurd words, retaining the tune and structure. Some schoolboys have put forward a revised version that readers may wish to sing at sporting events and state occasions:

Australians all eat ostriches
For we are young and free,
With cold and silent elephant oil,
Aroma skirt by sea.
A bounder lands in ancient skiffs
Of beauties rich and rare
On his three spades let every stage
Advance Australia Fair.
Enjoy a strange thin lettuce in
Advance Australia Fair.

While patriotism of the first type is confident and obvious, the second type is thoughtful and intuitive and involves unspoken contemplation of Australians' identity as a people. Just as the second type accounts for the fact that their chosen song celebrates a suicidal down and out, it manifests itself in the choice for a military commemoration, the anniversary of a failed and wasteful campaign, instead of a simplistic victory celebration like they have overseas.

Like the other leading writers and artists of his time, Banjo Paterson has been called a nationalist. He was very pleased when 'Waltzing Matilda' became a national song. But he and his contemporaries did not call themselves nationalists or try to make Australians more like foreigners in their patriotic expressions. In any case, even if nationalism was appropriate at the time of Federation or World War I, in Australia today it doesn't belong.

In its ethnic diversity Australia is much more than a nation; in its territorial spread and the variety of its resources, it is as comprehensive as a great empire; in its range of peoples and climates it is a whole continent; in its distinct position on the globe, it is the heartland of one of the world's major regions.

People like Archibald could see that our society would mature when it comes to terms with those conditions, and develops the human institutions appropriate to the assets at its disposal. This fact has since been forgotten. One of the missing elements is independent native culture, under local command, expressing distinctly Australian thought, thought such as we have in 'Waltzing Matilda'. A culture like that would form the basis of a distinct Australian civilisation, whereas a national chauvinism modelled on that of overseas countries stands in the way of such maturity.

IN THE DROVING DAYS

'Only a pound,' said the auctioneer,
'Only a pound; and I'm standing here
Selling this animal gain or loss.
Only a pound for the drover's horse;
One of the sort that was ne'er afraid,
One of the boys of the Old Brigade;
Thoroughly honest and game, I'll swear,
Only a little the worse for wear;
Plenty as bad to be seen in town,
Give me a bid and I'll knock him down;
Sold as he stands, and without recourse,
Give me a bid for the drover's horse.'

Loitering there in an aimless way
Somehow I noticed the poor old grey,
Weary and battered and screwed, of course,
Yet when I noticed the old grey horse,
The rough bush saddle, and single rein
Of the bridle laid on his tangled mane,
Straightway the crowd and the auctioneer
Seemed on a sudden to disappear,
Melted away in a kind of haze,
For my heart went back to the droving days.

Back to the road, and I crossed again
Over the miles of the saltbush plain—
The shining plain that is said to be

The dried-up bed of an inland sea,
Where the air so dry and so clear and bright
Refracts the sun with a wondrous light,
And out in the dim horizon makes
The deep blue gleam of the phantom lakes.

At dawn of day we would feel the breeze
That stirred the boughs of the sleeping trees,
And brought a breath of the fragrance rare
That comes and goes in that scented air;
For the trees and grass and the shrubs contain
A dry sweet scent on the saltbush plain.
For those that love it and understand,
The saltbush plain is a wonderland.
A wondrous country, where nature's ways
Were revealed to me in the droving days.

We saw the fleet wild horses pass,
And the kangaroos through the Mitchell grass,
The emu ran with her frightened brood
All unmolested and unpursued.
But there rose a shout and a wild hubbub
When the dingo raced for his native scrub,
And he paid right dear for his stolen meals
With the drovers' dogs at his wretched heels.
For we ran him down at a rattling pace,
While the pack horse joined in the stirring chase.
And a wild halloo at the kill we'd raise—
We were light of heart in the droving days.

'Twas a drover's horse, and my hand again
Made a move to close on a fancied rein.
For I felt the swing and the easy stride
Of the grand old horse that I used to ride
In drought or plenty, in good or ill,
That same old steed was my comrade still;
The old grey horse with his honest ways
Was a mate to me in the droving days.

When we kept our watch in the cold and damp,
If the cattle broke from the sleeping camp,
Over the flats and across the plain,
With my head bent down on his waving mane,
Through the boughs above and the stumps below
On the darkest night I would let him go
At a racing speed; he would choose his course,
And my life was safe with the old grey horse.
But man and horse had a favourite job,
When an outlaw broke from a station mob,
With a right good will was the stockwhip plied,
As the old horse raced at the straggler's side,
And the greenhide whip such a weal would raise,
We could use the whip in the droving days.

'Only a pound!' and this was the end—
Only a pound for the drover's friend.
The drover's friend that had seen his day,
And now was worthless, and cast away
With a broken knee and a broken heart

To be flogged and starved in a hawker's cart.
Well, I made a bid for a sense of shame
And the memories dear of the good old game.

'Thank you? Guinea! And cheap at that!
Against you there in the curly hat!
Only a guinea, and one more chance,
Down he goes if there's no advance,
Third, and the last time, one! two! three!'
And the old grey horse was knocked down to me.
And now he's wandering, fat and sleek,
On the lucerne flats by the Homestead Creek;
I dare not ride him for fear he'd fall,
But he does a journey to beat them all,
For though he scarcely a trot can raise,
He can take me back to the droving days.

Banjo Paterson, Bulletin, 20 June 1891

DANGERS OF DROWNING

BANJO PATERSON WAS A BORN CONSERVA-
tionist. Not much of a nature conservationist
certainly, but an ardent cultural conservationist.
The reader who dwells on the regretful tone in
poems like 'In the Droving Days' and 'On Kiley's
Run' might disparage his contribution as an inef-
fectual nostalgia, which merely achieves evocative
descriptions of old things that can't be recovered.

A broader view of his work reveals a different
truth. When Paterson sensed that something worthwhile or precious was endangered, his instinct was
not to preserve it in a museum cabinet, but to use
his art to keep it alive. We enjoy many cultural
assets that would have perished without him.

Hearing a rare and whimsical tune, with forgotten words, he 'decided it should have words to keep

it alive' and composed 'Waltzing Matilda'; in no time thousands had learnt it.

He nurtured words in the same way. The term 'waltzing matilda' was doomed to oblivion until it took his fancy and he decided to propagate it. Even 'jumbuck'—which almost no one says or writes— is understood everywhere, just because he liked it and wanted to keep it from extinction. These are not words that he used in his poems. There is a real-ness about the poems that compels both the poet and his characters to speak in natural English, in which sheep are 'sheep' and swags are 'swags'. 'Waltzing Matilda', as a work of whimsy, gave him a special chance to promote eccentric things, and to tip the scales in favour of the colourful option.

Words always fight with other words. Centuries ago the old word 'hound' lost its contest with the upstart 'dog'. It's not always the best word that wins—right now for instance, the good old word 'quilt' is being ousted by the ugly and effeminate 'doona'.

In Banjo's time a Latin word and an Aboriginal word for a kind of waterway were vying for one berth in the English language. Pitted against *anabranch*, the punters wouldn't have liked 'bill-abong's' chances of prevailing in the geography books; they might have forecast its gradual disap-pearance even from the vernacular. Then, thanks to the song, every school teacher had to be able to define billabong, and the mellifluous word that Banjo backed left the cold-blooded *anabranch* in its dust.

Now all over the cities and the beaches you see teenagers with 'Billabong' printed on their shirts and shorts and thongs. That of course is just a brand-name fad that may go the way of Craven-A and Ninja Turtles. But it's a fad that has claimed the generation that only knows computer games and McDonalds. They probably aren't thinking of the song when they buy the thongs, but the brand would never have been launched, let alone be popular, if 'Waltzing Matilda' hadn't prepared the way. Could there have been a clothing range called Anabranch instead, or would waterholes simply have been absent from fashion statements?

In an age of 'globalisation' the media and the education system flood the minds of new generations with market-driven British and US ideas and traditions. They learn very little about our own traditions and historical background.

But as long as 'Waltzing Matilda' continues to be sung, knowledgeable old people will go on explaining to curious young people what swagmen and squatters were, and there will be some kind of folk tradition, carrying knowledge of where they came from to those who miss out on it in their schooling: some idea perhaps that Australians had moulding experiences of their own, even before the Vietnam War.

The most solid labour of Banjo the conservationist appeared in 1905—his collection of *Old Bush Songs*. While folk songs were facing extinction all around him, like Noah he gathered them from their native environments, and he secured them on the printed page. 'The songs it contains are fast being forgotten,' he lamented in the Introduction. 'Thirty or forty years ago every station and every shearing shed had its singer, who knew some of the bush songs. Nowadays they are never sung.' He cites the example of 'Dunn, Gilbert and Ben Hall', a song from the upper Murrumbidgee about celebrated bushrangers:

> Thirty years ago everyone in the district had
> heard this song, and all the sympathizers
> with the bushrangers (which meant the bulk
> of the wild and scattered population) used to
> sing it on occasion; but today the most
> persistent enquiry has failed to reveal one
> man who can remember more than a few
> fragments of it; and yet it is only forty years
> since Ben Hall was shot. It is in the hope of
> rescuing these rough bush ballads from
> oblivion that the present collection is placed
> before the public.

The conservationist mission guides most of Banjo's poetry. He wanted the bush stories he enjoyed to live on. This is not the work of a historian; he saw no need to verify the facts and no harm in improving them. Like the poets of ancient Greece he took the story as worthwhile in itself, and a notable exploit as a thing to celebrate. The scenes he painted are useful to historians illustrating the world of their time. But it would give Banjo much more satisfaction to know that the man from Snowy River is a household word today, that there are still people who can tell you how Gilbert died or how Magee JP came to be christened Maginnis.

He prized the old bush life, and said so repeatedly, but he must have realised that in a changing world, he could not preserve it intact. The most he could aspire to would be the survival of some features, and some of the virtues of his bushmen.

As one of Archibald's brigade, he promoted and defended Australian ways, knowing that their future was so much in doubt that every hand at the pump made a difference.

The country you see when you look back to convict times is so alien that it's not really Australia at all, except as a geographical label. The Gold Rushes turned everything around, and Australia of the later decades of the nineteenth century is our country.

The people of those times, in the way they acted, felt, spoke and aspired, in what they took for granted and what they couldn't understand, were our people. There was an Australian character already strongly developed, as the English critic Francis Adams admitted in *Australian Essays*, even as he lamented the lack of Australian culture:

> In England the average man feels he is an inferior; in America he feels he is a superior; in Australia he feels he is an equal. This is indeed delightful. It is the first thing that strikes a new arrival in the country, and though Australia's sins—sins against true civilization I mean—are as many as they are heinous, still a multitude of them is covered by this; namely that here the people is neither servile nor insolent, but only shows its respect for itself by its respect for others.
>
> *Australian Essays*, London, 1886, p. 33

That trait of course is only one of a variety of characteristics that Australians today would be pleased to claim. It is surprising how many of the others are identified by writers who visited Australia in the 1870s and 1880s.

There was an Australian character, but there wasn't an Australian culture. Art, literature, music, theatre and architecture were just colonial reflections of European originals, British originals in particular. Obviously Aboriginal culture is an exception to this rule, but the white population had not managed to draw creative inspiration from it.

Without its own culture, the Australian character was an endangered species at risk of drowning in the run off from the Northern Hemisphere. But the 1880s and 1890s brought Archibald, Paterson, Lawson, Furphy, A. G. Stephens, the Lindsays, the Heidelberg School, the Federation movement and 'Waltzing Matilda', and it suddenly looked as if Australia was growing its own civilisation that would mature to become the peer of others such as European civilisation and American civilisation.

That seems like a natural progression. But the strong forces acting against it were obvious to Banjo and his fellow campaigners and it took their constant energy and vigilance to save the new Australian culture from going under.

'Waltzing Matilda' was a blow struck in that cause. Banjo made his thoughts on the matter obvious in 'The Old Australian Ways' (1902), the one and only poem he set in Britain. The voice is that of an Australian, sailing home, with the lights of England at his back. Suddenly, the Australian way is explicitly cast as the noble old tradition; the English way is the present and immediate threat, incompatible with the Australian spirit:

The narrow ways of English folk
Are not for such as we
They bear the long-accustomed yoke
Of staid conservancy:
But all our roads are new and strange
And through our blood there runs
The vagabonding love of change
That drove us westward of the range
And westward of the suns.

Vol. II, p. 142

The Englishman as the foreigner, ever ready to undermine the Australian way of life, had been a target of Archibald's *Bulletin* since the early 1880s. 'In those days all right-thinking people got their ideas, their boots, their shirts, their titles, their jobs, their political, moral and religious standards from England,' wrote Banjo, in the *Sydney Sportsman* on 25 January 1922. 'We were patronized by imported Governors, insulted by imported globetrotting snobs, exploited by imported actors and singers, mostly worn-out and incompetent. These people rode rough-shod over us, and we meekly submitted.' This was the climate in which Archibald and his crew set up their wall of sarcasm and outrage against the English.

When Australians back then saw people as a threat, it was the fashion to ridicule and disparage them, and nurture prejudices. Some, like Banjo, were too well mannered to indulge in strident racism and insults, but they all believed in the necessity of identifying Australians as better characters than other nationalities.

Paradoxically Archibald was an admirer and promoter of French culture. His enthusiasm was genuine, but it also made sense in his scheme: French culture was remote and did not threaten Australian ways; it could be welcomed and respected as a beneficial contribution and counter to English influence.

It is strange to remember that this English nation, so deplored by the new breed of Australian writer, and said to be lacking something we had in our very blood, was in recent generations ancestrally one with Australians; and hard to see how the people that sent out Marlborough and Captain Cook could be the same hopeless case their Australian descendents were writing about. The explanation was that the people who had remained in Britain were those who were content to have it for a home and complain about whatever they found unsatisfactory. Those who aspired to change left, and had their children in other countries.

> Our fathers came of roving stock
> That could not fixed abide:
> And we have followed field and flock

Since e'er we learnt to ride;
By miner's camp and shearing shed,
In land of heat and drought
We followed where our fortunes led,
With fortune always on ahead
And always farther out.

'The Old Australian Ways', vol. II, p. 142

Protected by this xenophobic attitude to the old country, fortunate in having creative genius about, Australia, in the late nineteenth century and early twentieth century, was able to lay down a really distinctive literature and to leave us with a shelf of classics to help underpin an independently vibrant civilisation in the ages to follow.

But after World War I, Australian civilisation as a project began to sink. It isn't enough to control the literary press and turn out a few bestsellers, because an initial surge of creative energy subsides in time. Every society with a durable, vigorous literature and culture of its own introduces it to rising generations as an essential strand in their education.

While the press and the bookshops offered fertile fields to truly Australian writing, the schools and universities remained tightly in the grasp of Englishmen and cringing Anglophiles. At school, children do not learn or recite Banjo Paterson's verses, or read Australian classics.

Classic literature comes from the ancient world, from Asia, from Europe and Australia, but in Australian schools it only comes from Britain and the USA. The only Australian books in schools are recent works that people won't even remember in thirty years' time. Schools teach British books that will be familiar for centuries to come.

The British, in their poets, in their favourite novelists, in Shakespeare, have a common literary currency linking all the generations. It keeps their culture intact through the ups and downs of history and creative vitality. But an Australian book is only taught to Australian pupils if it makes a pleasant, unchallenging read, with so little to explain that it's easy to teach.

Many Australian 'educators' believe that it doesn't matter what children are given—all they need is a text to work on. Others excuse their shoddy curriculum on the grounds that it must be relevant to today's concerns.

In learning, it's tomorrow's concerns that count and a classic, by definition, is relevant forever. Australian classics, even tested on today's issues, consistently have more to offer than books from Britain and books of the moment. Educators can't see the relevance of great Australian writers such as Banjo Paterson, Joseph Furphy, Vance Palmer, Eleanor Dark and Judah Waten and won't allow them in the classroom. Yet they go on teaching Keats and Browning, *Emma* and *Jane Eyre* and other books written for the BBC wardrobe department.

No 'vision splendid' is offered to Australian students. Instead they learn about building Jerusalem, 'in England's green and pleasant land'.

Banjo's works are excluded from the classroom, even though they are obviously the most attractive and instructive road into poetry for young readers, and offer the added advantage of familiarising them with their own culture and background. For more advanced study, teachers will naturally look for more testing poetry. Australian poets such as A. D. Hope, C. J. Dennis and Kenneth Slessor, are better than most of the American and British writers taught at this level.

Such is Life is probably the most challenging Australian classic. If you ask why it is so rarely taught, you'll be told that Furphy is too hard. But Furphy isn't as hard as James Joyce: they teach Joyce instead, because he's British.

A hundred years ago, British texts shared the classroom with a far broader range of literature than students meet today. Our ancestors learnt a wider variety of genres; they had Greek and Roman classics and the Bible as well. Unfortunately Britain then was at the summit of imperial pride—no longer ready to accept that it had anything to learn from other countries. Teachers of English succeeded in an offensive campaign to monopolise the literature curriculum. Australian schools and universities followed like sheep. They ditched Virgil—not for an Australian poet, but for Wordsworth.

The attitude underlying the complacency of the educators is called the cultural cringe: Australian isn't as good as imported. It's not a proposition that stands up when you look at the evidence—just an ignorant prejudice. 'Australia is a small country' they declare, contending that the home-grown product will rarely reach the highest standards.

Australia isn't small. It has three times the population of Shakespeare's Britain. Fifth-century Athens, that gave us Sophocles, Euripides, Aeschylus, Aristophanes, Socrates, Thucydides and Plato, had the same population as Wollongong. What achieves mediocrity is small mindedness. How would the Test side go, or the Olympic athletes, if they were taught that their country's small? That the only answer is to play like Englishmen? Fortunately sportspeople are more grown up in these matters than the intellectuals.

The cultural cringe now cowers behind an irresistible new banner. Whenever you lament the loss of something worthwhile developed by your own people, drowned in the waxing tide of US interests or British thinking, you will be reminded of the inevitability of 'globalisation'. To stand against globalisation is deemed at best an idiotic waste of time and, increasingly, a sin.

The case in favour of globalisation is a purely economic argument, founded on fundamentalist belief in the free market and the usefulness of the profit motive for maximising material wealth. No one demonstrates that globalisation of community values, mores, attitudes and beliefs, social health, literature and the arts is a good thing. There is no case at all for structuring the curriculum to undermine our own heritage, in order to achieve cultural globalisation.

In cultural matters globalisation is a deceitful euphemism for Americanisation and Anglicisation. True globalisation would introduce the great books of Europe, our rich literary heritage from the ancient world, the sophisticated writers of Asia and Australia. In British schools they'd be singing 'Waltzing Matilda' and teaching Miles Franklin and Joseph Furphy, just as readily as a Brontë sister is taught over here.

In Banjo's time the media that carried Australian culture were especially effective at reaching people: journals, books and local musical gatherings were the sources people went to for entertainment, inspiration and information.

TV, radio, recordings, computers and movies have taken over, deluging young Australians with

American culture. In place of quality Australian material, each new generation is raised on vacuous foreign drivel. There is no stopping it: American pulp is the opium we pacify our children with, having already allowed it to submerge our own minds in cultural apathy. But the profit motive that drives the entertainment media owns no authority in schools and universities. They should be turning towards distinguished Australian texts instead of marching away. Anyone who cares will be taking the teachers and authorities to task for their dereliction of duty, and trying to make them change.

Without a heritage of its own, Australia is doomed to be an outpost of empire. Without an Australian culture, the Australian character that emerged in the nineteenth century will die out and the people who live in Australia will be just a blend of British and American.

So far 'Waltzing Matilda' has been a liferaft: too catchy and memorable for the globalisers to sink, so it carries on Banjo's conservationist project. If things continue as they are, it too could go under eventually. In the 1960s almost every child could sing 'Waltzing Matilda'. It's not like that now and we can't assume that every future generation will get to hear the call from the billabong.

SEE FOR YOURSELF

TOURISTS TEND TO TRAVEL LIGHT, VISITING large areas with a few of their belongings and often only part of their mental powers; seeing the surface and the showpieces, coming home with nothing they didn't have already—except perhaps a souvenir key ring, a stubby holder or a funny tee-shirt.

This might explain why in half an hour you can learn more about a place from books than by talking all day long with someone who went as a tourist. There's the tourist dilemma: if the trip was just to use up time in long retirement years, to take advantage of the freedom between schooldays and a family, or to soak up some disposable income during a spot of leave, what was the good of it? Can there be any point in heading down the same old sheep track, to see what everyone else has seen and learn no more than all of them were told before you went?

Pilgrimage is a type of tourism that offers a yes answer, even to the myopic traveller. The dilemma may explain why there's been a decline in aimless peregrination, in walkabout and globe trotting, but not in pilgrimage—in journeys along significant paths to significant sites where something speaks to the pilgrim's soul, and supplies at least an answer to that question, what's the point?

Destinations offer themselves readily to the devout: holy places that nourish a spiritual need. But secular pilgrimage is burgeoning, and looking for shrines of its own. Many converge on Gallipoli, though it's rather far to go; the Kokoda Track has come into vogue, though costly and strenuous. Closer to home are Uluru, Sydney Cove, Glenrowan and so on.

'Waltzing Matilda' has that special significance that touches people, and a route and a locality for pilgrims. You too can head north for the outback, like Chris and Banjo. Long gone are regular boats to Rockhampton, but their rail journey is easily retraced. Rockhampton is now a midway point where the train from Brisbane to Longreach heads inland along the same rickety old Central Line they took in 1894 and 1895.

Queensland Railways calls this train *The Spirit of the Outback*—a gross misnomer for the plush and insulated moving world unto itself, devoid of dust, flies, mozzies, weather, discomfort and struggle. Each table in the dining car is named after an old sheep run, though there isn't a table for Dagworth. Dagworth is not a good name for tables.

So you must sit in the lounge with your drink and gaze out the window. Or lie in bed with the cabin lights off, and watch the moonlit trees go past, if you want any spirit to enter the experience. At Longreach there is no coach of Cobb and Co.'s, but a connecting bus keeps up the service and will get you along the bitumen to Winton in just over two hours. The Cobb and Co. timetable included an overnight stop, and in 1894 Constable Patrick Duffy broke the speed record by riding 200 km from Longreach to Winton in a single long day.

To see more, rather than catch the bus in Longreach, it is worth avoiding the wet season, and renting a four-wheel drive. Four driving wheels are more than enough in the flat country, but you need the ground clearance that comes with them. In Longreach there are car rental businesses, based at the aerodrome and ready to meet the train.

Winton has camping grounds, motels and pubs. Its town water supply is of special note. The water comes from 4000 feet below the surface, at a temperature of 80 degrees. It sits in a dam to cool off to a less dangerous heat before being piped to the hot taps all over town. There are no hot-water heaters; instead, a well-equipped house has a cool-water tank and the luxury of cold taps. Wintonites speak enthusiastically of their water, its purity, ideal mineral content and beneficial qualities. This positive attitude is a tribute to their indomitable spirit; or else a lifetime of imbibing has inured them to its taste and smell—the worst smell of any town water in the world.

They will tell you all you need to do is boil the water or let it sit a while, to eliminate the awful taste, but alas, they have no idea. Every water drinker who visits must carry water from elsewhere, and it's a good idea for you to hold your breath while showering. An outsider might wonder why they don't replace the cool-water tanks with rainwater tanks. But they wouldn't understand.

In the 500 km from Longreach to Cloncurry, Winton is the only urban centre—but it isn't an imposing town, and now as always its glory is its pubs, which dominate the streetscape and carry on the town's traditions.

In the median strip of Elderslie Street, between the Australian Hotel and Tattersalls, is a waterhole flanked by pelicans in bronze. Further up, a bronze swagman tends his fire in front of the swimming pool, near where the Post Office Hotel used to be.

This was the pub owned by Marie Riley's mother, where Herbert Ramsey sang 'Waltzing Matilda' to the Governor. Behind the pool, on Vindex Street, is the block where Aloha used to stand—the home of Fred and Marie Riley, where 'Waltzing Matilda' was played on the piano and sung for the first time in town. Across Elderslie Street from the pool, Banjo Paterson stands in bronze before the Waltzing Matilda Centre, the main attraction for visitors. Included in the Centre is the old Quantilda Museum, named for the airline and the song that Winton launched on the world. The history of the district is instructively presented there.

The Centre includes an indoor billabong with statues and a show on tape and film. But you might find the highlight is the hall set up behind it where by pushing little buttons you can listen to the song in a range of different versions, as often as you like. The varying renditions are endlessly fascinating, each with a charm of its own. The oldest, sung by an anonymous Queenslander in 1927, is idiosyncratic and quick. Edna Everage's interpretation is one of the most popular. The same can't be said for Bill Haley and the Comets—their button has been vandalised, presumably by someone who couldn't bear it, and now they can't be heard.

Avoiding partiality, the Centre plays arrangements of both the Cloncurry tune, and the popular tune derived from Marie Cowan. Up the street, on the pianola at the North Gregory Hotel, you can hear a fine old arrangement by Edith Murn, again derived from Cowan. What they don't have in Winton is the 1895 tune, the original from Chris Macpherson, which Banjo clothed in words. There isn't a statue of Chris Macpherson, but that seems a small omission compared to the loss of her melody.

Tradition names the North Gregory Hotel as the venue where the song was first performed in public. The North Gregory today is the fourth building on the site where Corfield first established it in 1879. The third burnt down in 1946. In a town of pubs, the North Gregory was the pride and joy, but after the fire no business came forward with the capital to build.

To cope with the crisis the Shire of Winton successfully approached the Queensland Parliament for authority to build and run its own hotel. Many a community has expressed its communal spirit in a monumental project, a showpiece to the world: a shrine or a museum, a temple or cathedral, or perhaps a home of learning. Disdaining commonplaces of that sort, Winton expressed its true character by putting up a pub in solid brick.

In its vintage 1950s architecture, this Taj Mahal of Winton doesn't look as good to some as the nice old 1920s building it replaced.

From the people of the town and district the Shire raised a sum embarrassingly large, and opened up a pub. The Shire ran it at a loss, as a lesson to the world in what a hotel ought to be; for its guests there were room service, bellhops and waiters, with silver service in the dining room. According to Graham Strang, whose family runs the hotel today, before dawn every morning staff used to get up and repolish the timber floors.

After sale to private ownership, it gradually degenerated to become a normal country pub. In 1998 the Strang family, on nearby Drumlion, sold up their property and bought the North Gregory, aiming to restore some at least of the old prestige. Nowadays, they get passing tour groups to sing 'Waltzing Matilda' to the pianola music, in a room festooned with memorabilia, watched over by a portrait of an aging Banjo Paterson.

The bitumen now goes all the way from Winton to Cloncurry—renamed for pilgrims, 'The Matilda Highway'. The road at last is excellent, but the traffic that would have used it is largely gone. While some districts of inland Queensland are fairly static in their population, and some places like Longreach have grown and thrived, the Waltzing Matilda district has declined in activity, and Winton and the country around it are depopulated. A labour-intensive wool industry has given way to beef cattle, so the great seasonal influx of workers to the stations, and drinkers to the pubs, is now a thing of the past. Quietness reigns, punctuated by road trains and spoilt in the calm of evening by mozzies. Winton, and Kynuna, and surrounding rural properties are homes to fewer people than they were in recent decades. But they are still lived in and looked after: the tiny settlements by the roadside and railway, still marked on maps, are completely defunct. Not even a shed remains at most of them and on the trip to Kynuna from Winton you may not see a soul.

This isn't the place to expand on the many rewards unconnected to 'Waltzing Matilda' that the region offers visitors—such as the impressive birds and animals, and the haunting beauty of the scenery, especially where rising over the plain are low hills that must be all that remains of a higher terrain eroded away aeons ago. The weather is usually pleasant; the locals, though scarce, are jovial and helpful, and blessed with a sense of history. Winton is the nearest town to Lark Quarry, where a famous mob of dinosaurs left its many footprints preserved forever in rock that set after the dinosaurs passed. Coincidentally, Banjo thought he would be famous for the same reason:

Such writers as Henry Lawson and myself had the advantage of writing in a new country. In

all museums throughout the world one may
see plaster casts of the footprints of weird
animals, footprints preserved for posterity,
not because the animals were particularly
good of their sort but because they had the
luck to walk on the lava while it was
cooling. There is just a faint hope that
something of the sort will happen to us.

'Looking Backward', 1938, vol. II, p. 759

Kynuna is just a few buildings plonked beside the
highway. After all these years the hotel is still in business, although its buildings don't look permanent,
and it has been renamed The Blue Heeler, after the
famous dog. Here it was that Bob Macpherson, in
a shout that included Richard Magoffin's grandfather, had his heart attack and died in 1930. You
can still see the internal window into the public bar,
where Bob Macpherson handed in champagne for
the union shearers in 1895. Empty and neglected a
little further up the road is the old Matilda Expo
building, where Magoffin used to preach the truth
against the infidels at Winton.

Like Bob Macpherson and the troopers three
in September 1894, you can travel back along the
Diamantina River to the sites that have a role in the
making of the song.

Of these sites, only Combo is signposted, so you'll need to get directions at Kynuna, and preferably a sketch map. A few miles out of town along dirt roads and tracks is a pair of billabongs where the renegade shearers camped in 1894. You can see that the one where Frenchy Hoffmeister shot himself still has a little island in the middle, with a coolibah tree living on it. Further down, Combo waterhole, which tradition associates with the song, is one of a series of waterholes, reached by a foot track that is clearly marked. The track crosses a number of impressive overshots, which are weirs with gently sloping sides in a course of the river, beautifully and ingeniously surfaced in local stone— a hot and back-breaking labour skilfully performed by Chinese workers in the early 1890s. Banjo would have been shown them by the Macphersons, who must have spent a lot of money to put them in. Their purpose was to make artificial billabongs, so that when the river ceases to flow there is still a good supply of water for stock. Being on the boundary of Kynuna station and Dagworth, it is said to have been a picnic spot where the squatting families met. And being just inside the boundaries of Winton shire, it has been declared a reserve, adorned with noticeboards for tourists. In fact its links with the song are probably only incidental.

Further down again, several hundred metres away from a side road to the river, is the site of the old Dagworth homestead where 'Waltzing Matilda' was conceived. There's little there to look at now—just a few timbers in the ground and a bit of a stone floor.

The closest you can get to the Waltzing Matilda experience is to select a congenial billabong and camp by it. There are plenty of coolibah trees to choose from and wood lying around to boil a billy. To turn up with an empty tuckerbag would be carrying authenticity too far, and to wait for a jumbuck to come and drink, a vain expectation. For readers who are free of the cares and hardships that sent men on the wallaby, camping by a billabong can be a jolly experience; they may even be moved to break into song and hopefully will not miss the opportunity to contemplate the wondrous glory of the everlasting stars.

HIS GHOST MAY
BE HEARD

SINCE THE SWAGMAN GOT HIS BILLY
going that day under the coolibah, we've had the
Olympic Games, Federation, nine wars, the Depression, aviation, TV, the Sixties, Rap music and a six-
fold increase in population.

Through all that the call still comes loud and
clear from the billabong: 'Who'll come a-waltzing
matilda with me?'

More loud than clear actually. There's still plenty
of room for doubt about what it is really saying to
us. How could it still speak significantly to anyone
at all in a changed world, after all this time?

But there you have it. People of every new generation are enchanted by 'Waltzing Matilda' and
respond to it as though it were new and immediate.
A phenomenon like that is a sign of qualities that

survive in people through the vicissitudes of time and space: qualities worth keeping in a hard, competitive world, because they make us what we are.

You may not be able to come up with a sensible explanation. You may only know that it counts because it is one of the things that make the hair stand up on the back of your neck, or it sets images going round in your mind long after the singing subsides. Not being able to translate that into words doesn't mean it's false or pointless; music and poetry mine into real and permanent assets that lie beyond the reach of reports and lessons, or simple wants and needs.

Obviously in a complex, shifting world some changes are for the better and some for the worse. When millions cling tenaciously to a song, without being told to—a song that for all its matter-of-fact relevance should have dropped out of fashion a hundred years ago—it conjures up things of value that we can't afford to lose.

In a world of literal meanings, 'Waltzing Matilda' points below the surface to deeper understanding. In a prose world, the poetry and music override one's concentration on mundane objects. A workforce that dedicates every waking hour to productivity is reminded of an age—bygone or imaginary—when people sang and waited for their tea.

To today's generations who take themselves very seriously, and try to do everything by the book, the voice from the billabong offers a contrary perspective on which of their concerns matter in the great scheme of things.

WALTZING MATILDA

Once a jolly swagman camped by a billabong
Under the shade of a coolibah tree,
And he sang as he watched and waited till his billy boiled
'Who'll come a-waltzing Matilda with me?'

'Waltzing Matilda, waltzing Matilda,
Who'll come a-waltzing Matilda with me?'
And he sang as he watched and waited till his billy boiled
'Who'll come a-waltzing Matilda with me?'

Down came a jumbuck to drink at the billabong:
Up jumped the swagman and grabbed him with glee.
And he laughed as he stowed that jumbuck in his
      tuckerbag,
'You'll come a-waltzing Matilda with me.'

'Waltzing Matilda, waltzing Matilda,
You'll come a-waltzing Matilda with me.'
And he laughed as he stowed that jumbuck in his
      tuckerbag,
'You'll come a-waltzing Matilda with me.'

Down came the squatter, mounted on his thoroughbred;
Down came the troopers, one, two, three:
'Whose is that jumbuck you've got in your tuckerbag?
You'll come a-waltzing Matilda with me.'

'Waltzing Matilda, waltzing Matilda,
You'll come a-waltzing Matilda with me.
Whose is that jumbuck you've got in your tuckerbag?
You'll come a-waltzing Matilda with me.'

Up jumped the swagman and dived into the billabong;
'You'll never catch me alive!' said he;
And his ghost may be heard as you pass by that
    billabong,
'Who'll come a-waltzing Matilda with me?'

'Waltzing Matilda, waltzing Matilda,
Who'll come a-waltzing Matilda with me?'
And his ghost may be heard as you pass by that
    billabong,
'Who'll come a-waltzing Matilda with me?'

                              A modern version

Appendix 1: The Music

The chapter 'Centuries in the Making' mentions that historians are sceptical about 'The Bold Fusilier'. It seems there is no knowledge of 'The Bold Fusilier' in England that could not have come from Australians enquiring in connection with 'Waltzing Matilda'. Other than its historical setting, the only indications that it existed before 'Waltzing Matilda' come from twentieth-century recollections. Richard Magoffin is convinced that 'The Bold Fusilier' is a parody of 'Waltzing Matilda'. His view is based on statements by Herb Young, a Boer War veteran, to the Desaillys of Fairview station (near Dagworth). Young remembered 'Waltzing Matilda' being performed at a concert by Australian troops in South Africa during the Boer War, to an audience that included English Fusiliers. He recalled the English including 'The Bold Fusilier' in their own concert soon afterwards. As theirs was the later concert the English might have put new words to the Waltzing Matilda tune.

Two difficulties arise. Firstly, if at the English concert 'The Bold Fusilier' was new and Australians heard it for the first time, it is hard to account for the fact that the song was so much better known in Australia than England. Secondly, in the structure of its lines, 'The Bold Fusilier' is remarkably close to Marie Cowan's 'Waltzing Matilda', drafted in 1903, after the War, but not so close to the 'Waltzing Matilda' drafted by Banjo Paterson in 1895, the song that would have been taken to the War by the Queenslanders.

It is easier to believe that two different songs existed—the old 'Bold Fusilier' and the new 'Waltzing Matilda'. Their similarity might have encouraged the English troops to respond to one with the other; and have caused the songs to grow closer as time passed. If so, 'The Bold Fusilier' must have influenced Marie Cowan, and perhaps Harry Nathan, as they worked on their arrangements.

Some traditions live on in colonised lands, after dying out in their mother countries. In Austria, bread rolls used to be baked in a crescent shape to commemorate victory over the Turks in the seventeenth century. The crescent roll spread to France, and with French colonists to Canada. In France it disappeared, replaced by the modern croissant, which is not like bread. But in Canada it survived to our own time. In the USA and Canada on Hallowe'en children dress in scary costumes and beg for cakes and lollies door to door. This custom was introduced by British colonists but then virtually disappeared in Britain. Apparently marketing people have recently had success in reintroducing it.

Similarly, if 'The Bold Fusilier' is genuinely very old, its being known better in Australia, or only in Australia, is understandable on the basis that it came in colonial times and was kept alive, while being forgotten or almost forgotten in England.

In Chapter 10 of *On the Origins of Waltzing Matilda* Harry Pearce introduces Kathleen Cooper who recounts that her grandfather, Henry Bushby, sang 'The Bold Fusilier', having learnt it from his grandfather, George Bushby (born c.1760). Henry taught her the first verse and chorus, but her grandmother objected. 'There were several verses, probably ribald and not taught to children,' Mrs Cooper wrote. The Bushbys came from West Tarring, 100 km from Rochester. Victoria's first permanent white settlers, the Hentys, who founded Portland, west of Warrnambool, were landowners in West Tarring. Another old family in that locality was the Chippers, known according to Mrs Cooper for their musical skills and the traditional repertoire they preserved. She refers to one of their old songs as 'Ring the Bell Watchman', to the same music as 'Click Go the Shears'. Coming to Australia in 1829, James Henty brought labourers and servants from West Tarring, including John and Mary Chipper and George and Marie Bushby, with two Bushby children. Chippers had lived for centuries in the West Tarring area; in sixteenth-century church records they were the minstrels. For information on the Hentys' servants, Pearce relies on Marnie Basset's book *The Hentys: An Australian Colonial Tapestry* (1954).

If 'The Bold Fusilier' and 'Ring the Bell Watchman' are authentically antique, it's easy to see how they took root in early colonial Australia and contributed to 'Waltzing Matilda' and 'Click Go the Shears'.

These songs are relatively modern in character, not typical of the eighteenth century. This has been used to challenge claims that 'The Bold Fusilier' predates 'Waltzing Matilda' and comes from Marlborough's time. But it is probably irrelevant, because no eighteenth-century songs have reached recent generations by oral transmission without taking on modern characteristics and shedding eighteenth-century characteristics.

Another objection to 'The Bold Fusilier's' antiquity is that it does not appear in the comprehensive collections of English folk songs compiled during the last couple of centuries. But that does not support the conclusion that it did not exist in England before World War I. These collections routinely omit songs that offended conventional morality including drinking songs, slanders, blasphemies and bawdy or obscene songs. The fact that only the first verse and chorus of 'The Bold Fusilier' are remembered is a strong indication that it was too bawdy or obscene to publish.

And there is still the mystery that Marie Cowan's melody appears like a composite of 'The Bold Fusilier' and Chris Macpherson's—not easily explained if 'The Bold Fusilier' is a parody of a pre-Cowan version.

These arguments all combined still do not prove a case. I think 'The Bold Fusilier' is likely to be very old; and inspired by a continental European tune; while it probably reached its present form under modern influences, including the influence of 'Waltzing Matilda', there were probably rhythmic and melodic resemblances to begin with. Today's popular tune of 'Waltzing Matilda'—in essence the Cowan of 1903—is likely to have been strongly influenced by 'The Bold Fusilier'.

Those who disagree include people whose views cannot lightly be discounted: the late Richard Magoffin; the folk musician Dave de Hugard, who has made a study of 'Waltzing Matilda'; and the National Library's curator of music, Robyn Holmes, who is an expert on the Waltzing Matilda music.

The musical history is complicated by the National Archives' Harry Nathan manuscript, with a melody like Marie Cowan's of 1903. Because the document is dated 1905, it can be explained logic-ally by stating that Nathan must have made Marie

Cowan's music the basis of a new arrangement. On the cover sheet Nathan has written: 'This composition of music entirely by Harry A. Nathan. Copyright deferred. To my old friend W. A. Renwick, 10th August, 1905. Composed 1900, copyright 1903'. This has been taken as proof that Nathan composed the popular melody in 1900. If true, Marie Cowan must have got hold of it somehow in 1903. If things moved very quickly, Nathan's tune might even have reached South Africa in time to inspire the fusiliers. I don't accept any of this. Nathan's meaning is ambiguous, but his manuscript looks just like an arrangement based on Cowan's work, which is probably the 1903 copyright he refers to. He probably means that he has deferred copyright on this 1905 arrangement of his.

Appendix 2:
Notes about Sources
and Further Reading

Vol. I in references throughout the book stands for *Singer of the Bush*, the first volume of *A. B. 'Banjo' Paterson: Complete Works*; Vol. II is *Song of the Pen*, the second volume of *A. B. 'Banjo' Paterson: Complete Works*.

National Library papers referred to in these notes are in the manuscript collection: NLA MS 9753 and MS 9065.

WALTZING MATILDA COUNTRY. Information about **initial settlement** is from Corfield's *Reminiscences of Queensland* and P. and S. Forrest, *Winton*. I believe Morrison's reports in the *Age* of 1883 are the only published notice of **John Smith**. For **Morrison**, see Paterson's interview, vol. II, p. 163; C. Pearl, *Morrison of Peking*; and G. Morrison, *An Australian in China*. His reports in the *Times* of 13 and 15 June 1900 are a readable and fascinating account of the **Boxer Uprising**, extracted in *War in Words*. For the opulent **squatter families** of Victoria and their *Land Act* troubles, see A. Selzer, *The Armytages of Como*.

UP CAME THE SQUATTERS. Verses 2 to 8 are extracted from 'The Gumsucker's Dirge', complete in

Joseph Furphy, pp. 386–7. Furphy's *Such is Life* is a detailed and illuminating fictional treatment of relations between station people and itinerants.

THE COMPOSER AND THE POET. For the **Macphersons**, see Magoffin's *Fair Dinkum Matilda* and *Waltzing Matilda: Song of Australia*. **Christina Macpherson's** visits to Meningoort are reported in a letter from A. J. McIntosh to Richard Magoffin, 10 October 1968. **Mad Dan Morgan** figures in every general book on bushranging. **Banjo's life**, see C. Semmler, *Banjo of the Bush*. **'Clancy of the Overflow'** is in his first book, *The Man from Snowy River and other Verses*, 1895. For **Archibald** see, inter alia, P. Rolfe, *The Journalistic Javelin* and S. Lawson, *The Archibald Paradox*. His **letter to Banjo** (25 January 1922) is quoted in vol. II, p. 432. For Banjo's and **Kipling's** correspondence with **George Robertson**, see *George Robertson*. The **popularity of Banjo and Kipling** is reported by Tony Barker in *George Robertson*. **Paterson's poetics**, including the sentences quoted, are stated most fully in 'Singers among Savages' (vol. II, p. 561), a talk given in the 1930s. See also 'Kipling's Work' (vol. II, p. 507). As early as 1905 it is clear, from the Introduction to *Old Bush Songs*, that he suspected that Aboriginal poetry is highly sophisticated, and worth studying. In envisaging poetry as primaeval and biological he is not completely without fellows among critics, even if he never knew of them. 'Here is a new born baby whose eyes cannot yet turn and whose fists cannot yet stretch out, but who, extending his arms and twisting his feet utters a sound from his mouth.

When I look at it carefully I find this is really poetry', wrote Jin Sheng Tarn (d. 1661) (translated in J. Y. Liu, *The Art of Chinese Poetry*, University of Chicago Press, Chicago, 1962, p. 74). Paterson wrote, 'Even the lower animals seem to have this instinct…certain varieties of frogs run a very definite chorus. You will hear one old fellow booming out the solo while the rest take up the refrain. In my opinion these were the primeval beginnings of poetry, but I won't ask you to go back as far as the frogs' (vol. II, p. 56). Jin Sheng Tarn and Paterson have very different applications for their similar notions; Jin goes on to disparage formal rules of metrical verse; Paterson is a leading exponent of formal, metrical versification.

SWAGMEN. The fullest version of 'Click Go the Shears' is in Stewart's and Keesing's *Old Bush Songs*. Like most folk songs it exists in many variants; it is quoted here as I heard it in childhood. **Christina's letter** to Wood and the burning of **Dagworth shed** are in the National Library papers, and Magoffin's books.

THE LONG LONG ARM OF THE LAW. The account of **Hoffmeister's demise** and the enquiry is based on the three Magoffin books in the bibliography, and the Magoffin papers in the National Library, NLA MS 9753.

MAKING A SONG and **WHAT DOES IT MEAN?** The **movements and doings** of participants in these chapters are documented in many first-hand and secondary accounts, riddled with minor discrepancies.

They are in books listed in the bibliography and the National Library papers. Eight locations have been nominated as the place where 'Waltzing Matilda' was **first sung** and/or first sung publicly. The Forrests (*Vision Splendid*, p. 96) reveal a newspaper report that **Sarah Riley** went up from Melbourne late in May 1895. They are sure this would have been her only trip to Winton that year, which if correct undermines the traditional chronology of her joint excursion to Dagworth with Banjo, and the view of the other writers that the two were there together early in the year. It raises doubts about claims that the song debuted early in 1895 and that Banjo helped settle **labour strife**. Magoffin believes Banjo made six trips to the district in 1895–96. Various opinions are clearer than the evidence on these matters. At the latest, Banjo was on the scene soon after the strife, because in 'Golden Water' he reports that he was present when the Macphersons passed champagne to the strikers through the pub window—an event that took place at **Kynuna Hotel** early in 1895. Either Sarah Riley made more than one visit to Queensland that year, or Banjo went there first without her. 'Golden Water' is in vol. II, p. 498. **Banjo's comments to Kelly** are in Kelly's review of Manifold's *Who Wrote the Ballads* in the *Sun*, c. 1964 (NLA MS 9753 box 1, folder 1). There are two **manuscripts** in Paterson's hand, words only, perhaps from 1895, and two in Christina's hand, words and music, undated. Copies are at the National Library or in the Library's 'National Treasures' travelling exhibition. **Helen Anderson's memories of Paterson** were recorded in a statement to Richard

Magoffin in 1966. **German origins** of the words and custom of waltzing matilda are revealed in detail by Pearce in Part I of *On the Origins of Waltzing Matilda*. The complete text of *An Outback Marriage*, also titled *In No Man's Land*, is in vol. I. **'Freedom on the Wallaby'** exists in several versions; what I believe is the original is quoted here from C. Roderick's edition of *Henry Lawson Poems*. Magoffin's description of what the **swagman** represents is from *The Provenance of Waltzing Matilda*, p. 4. Peter Forrest's objections to a **political reading** and connecting actual events and people to 'Waltzing Matilda' are from *Vision Splendid*, p. 104. 'Waltzing Matilda' fans will find **Nasrudin's** actions entertaining, instructive and easily accessible in Shah's *The Exploits of the Incomparable Mulla Nasrudin*. **Geoff Willats-Bryan**: interviewed April 2006.

CENTURIES IN THE MAKING. 'Thou Bonnie Wood of Craigielee' was published in *Miniature Museum of Scotch Songs and Music*, Edinburgh, 1818. **Helen Anderson's memories of 'Craigielee'** are in her letter to Richard Magoffin, 7 July 1968. References to **Pearce** are to Chapters 9, 10 and 11 of *On the Origins of Waltzing Matilda*. The Billy Tea leaflet with **Marie Cowan's** words and music is in the National Library and illustrated in Magoffin's books.

FROM THE BILLABONG TO THE WORLD. Banjo's newspaper reports from the **Boer War** are collected in vol. I. Comments of **Winston Churchill**, John **Williamson** and **Slim Dusty** are displayed at the

Waltzing Matilda Centre. **'And the Band Played Waltzing Matilda'** is quoted from *101 Australian Songs for the Guitar*. The **Latin translation** is quoted in Semmler's *Banjo of the Bush,* credited to Xavier College magazine. **Paul Keating's speech** is quoted in *'Men and Women of Australia'*, p. 52.

UP JUMPED THE EXPERTS. For fans of 'Waltzing Matilda' with an appetite for more substantial poetry after Banjo's work, the *Iliad* is ideal. Several translations are readily available; the main thing is to avoid a prose translation, which masks the impact and delicacy of the three-level narrative and complex characterisation. **E. J. Brady's letter** is quoted in Mendelsohn's *A Waltz with Matilda,* and by Semmler. **Oscar Mendelsohn's** comments on Paterson's 'dishonesty' are from *A Waltz with Matilda,* p. 13. The **A. A. Phillips** quote is from *Meanjin,* vol. 3, 1965. **Therese Radic's** statements are from *Journal of Australian Studies,* vol. 49, pp. 40, 42 and 45. **Magoffin's** complaint against Radic and the Waltzing Matilda Centre is set out in *The Provenance of Waltzing Matilda.* 'Waltzing Matilda' is not unusual in drawing controversy over **political readings and allegorical interpretation.** Enchanted by the beauty of old works, but detached from the circumstances in which they were created, modern critics are irritated by what they see as attempts to shackle them to non-artistic purposes. China's oldest anthology, *The Book of Poetry,* is at the centre of a similar dispute, as modern Westerners ridicule the ancient commentators who point at political allegories. In cases of this sort readers can get most from old works by standing back enough to see that they validly carry multiple readings. **Peter and Sheila Forrest on Paterson's prominence:** *Vision Splendid*, p. 104.

ANTHEMS AND NATIONALISM. McCormick is said to have penned four verses of 'Advance Australia Fair' in 1878; verse 2 I quote from *101 Australian Songs for the Guitar*; verses 3 and 4 seem to have died out.

DANGERS OF DROWNING. Francis Adams is quoted in Vance Palmer's *The Legend of the Nineties*, p. 28. Others with early accounts of the **Australian character** are Anthony Trollope, Mark Twain, Richard Twopeny and J. A. Froude. For readers not yet exposed to the superior qualities of **classic Australian writing**, editions of the authors named in this chapter can be ordered through all good book shops and libraries. Leigh Dale's *The English Men* surveys English domination in Australian **universities**.

SEE FOR YOURSELF. The history of the **North Gregory Hotel** comes partly from Graham Strang, interviewed April 2006.

Bibliography

The Australian Encyclopaedia, Angus and Robertson, Sydney, 1958.

Barker, A. W., *George Robertson: A Publishing Life in Letters*, University of Queensland Press, Brisbane, 1982.

Barker, A. W., *When Was That*, John Ferguson, Sydney, 1988.

Barnes, J. (ed.), *Joseph Furphy*, University of Queensland Press, Brisbane, 1981.

Corfield, W. H., *Reminiscences of Queensland 1862–1899*, A. H. Frater, Brisbane, 1921.

Dale, L., *The English Men*, Association for the Study of Australian Literature, Toowoomba, 1997.

Dennis, C. J., *The Complete Sentimental Bloke*, ed. N. James, A & R Classics, Sydney, 2001.

Dennis, C. J., *The Moods of Ginger Mick*, Angus and Robertson, Sydney, 1916.

Forrest, P. & S., *Vision Splendid*, Winton Shire Council and Winton and District Historical Society and Museum, Winton, Qld, 2005.

Fullilove, M. (ed.), *'Men and Women of Australia' Our Greatest Modern Speeches*, Random House, Sydney, 2005.

Furphy, J., *The Annotated Such is Life*, Halstead Classics, Sydney, 1999.

Gardner, H., 'Matilda's Mice', *Australian Tradition*, Aug/Sep 1994, reprinted in *The Cornstalk Gazette*, no. 247, 1994, p. 26.

Lawson, S., *The Archibald Paradox*, Melbourne University Press, Melbourne, 1983, 2006 edn.

Lindsay, N., *Bohemians at the Bulletin*, Angus and Robertson, Sydney, 1965.

Magoffin, R., *Fair Dinkum Matilda*, Mimosa Press, Charters Towers, 1973.

Magoffin, R., *The Provenance of Waltzing Matilda*, Matilda Expo, Kynuna, Qld, 2001.

Magoffin, R., *Waltzing Matilda: Song of Australia*, Mimosa Press, Charters Towers, 1983.

Manifold, J. S., *Who Wrote the Ballads?*, Australasian Book Society, Sydney, 1964.

May, S., *The Story of Waltzing Matilda*, Smith and Paterson, Brisbane, 1944.

Mendelsohn, O., *A Waltz with Matilda*, Lansdowne, Melbourne, 1966.

101 Australian Songs for the Guitar, Wise Publications, Sydney, 2004.

Paterson A. B. (ed.), *Old Bush Songs*, Angus and Robertson, Sydney, 1905 (Penguin edn, Melbourne, 2006).

Paterson, A. B., *Singer of the Bush: A. B. 'Banjo' Paterson: Complete Works 1885–1900*, Sydney, 1983; Redwood edn, Melbourne, 2000 (vol. I).

Paterson, A. B., *Song of the Pen: A. B. 'Banjo' Paterson: Complete Works 1901–1941*, Sydney, 1983; Redwood edn, Melbourne, 2000 (vol. II).

Pearce, H. H., *On the Origins of Waltzing Matilda*, Hawthorn Press, Melbourne, 1971.

Radic, T., 'The Songlines of Waltzing Matilda', *Journal of Australian Studies*, vol. 49, 1996, p. 39.

Richardson, M. E. (ed.), *War in Words: The Halstead Armoury of Australian War Writing*, Halstead Classics, Sydney, 2004.

Roderick, C., *Banjo Paterson*, Allen and Unwin, Sydney, 1993.

Rolfe, P., *The Journalistic Javelin*, Sydney, 1980.

Selzer, A., *The Armytages of Como*, Halstead, Sydney, 2003.

Semmler, C., *The Banjo of the Bush*, University of Queensland Press, Brisbane, 1966 (2nd edn, 1974).

Shah, I., *The Exploits of the Incomparable Mulla Nasrudin*, Picador edn, London, 1973.

Stewart, D. & Keesing, N. (eds), *Old Bush Songs*, Sydney, 1957; A & R Australian Classics edn, Sydney, 1976.

Voltaire, J. F. M. A. de, *Le Siècle de Louis XIV*, Berlin, 1751; 1753 edn. tr. M. P. Pollack, *The Age of Louis XIV*, Everyman, London, 1926.

Wilde, W. H., Hooton, J. & Andrews, B., *The Oxford Companion to Australian Literature*, Oxford University Press, Melbourne 1985.

Wilkes, G. A., *Dictionary of Australian Colloquialisms*, Sydney University Press, Sydney, 1978.

Acknowledgements

Before this book was finished, we lost our leading expert on 'Waltzing Matilda', with the death of Richard Magoffin. It is his research that makes possible an adequate account of the song's origins; even his critics depend on it. His help at a difficult time deserves thanks which I can no longer pass on.

I have also to thank my wife Carolyn for her careful attention to the text, my mother Grace for her commitment to the project and my son Jack who made up for my musical handicaps. I have taken advantage of many people's insights, without being able to name them all; particularly though, Geoff Willats-Bryan of the Waltzing Matilda Centre, and Robyn Holmes, curator of music at the National Library, and Dave de Hugard of Maldon, Vic., who are the most knowledgeable people on the music, were generous with their time and knowledge. For their practical help, I thank James Peterson of Canberra, Bill Magoffin of Sydney, Wendy Skilbeck the editor, and my colleagues Alana Ayliffe and Catherine Retter. I am especially grateful to Foong Ling Kong of Melbourne University Press, without whose vision this book would not exist.

M. E. Richardson, Warrimoo, NSW, 2006

Index of People